MW01610663

WALKS IN
Perth
OUTDOORS

GOVERNMENT OF
WESTERN AUSTRALIA

DEPARTMENT OF
Conservation
AND LAND MANAGEMENT
Conserving the nature of WA

Healthy Parks
Healthy People

© Department of Conservation and Land Management 2005
First published 1993
Reprinted with amendments 1996
Completely revised in 2000
Reprinted with amendments 2005

Publisher: Department of Conservation and Land Management, Dick Perry Avenue, Kensington, Western Australia, 6151.
Editor of the first two editions: David Gough.
Editor of third and fourth editions: Carolyn Thomson-Dans.
Features: John Hunter and David Gough.
Design: Sue Marais.
Production: Tiffany Taylor.
Cover photography: Robert Garvey.
Illustrations and location maps: Gooitzen van der Meer.
Mud maps*: Louise Burch.
Editorial assistance: Verna Costello.
Marketing: Estelle de San Miguel.

*The mud maps and text are based on information provided by Department of Conservation and Land Management staff and volunteers.

Acknowledgments:
To the Department of Conservation and Land Management staff in the Swan Region, Regional Parks and the Tracks and Trails Unit, especially Annie Keating; the staff of Whiteman Park; the Friends of Star Swamp, particularly David Pike; the Friends of Trigg Bushland Reserve, particularly Steve Tulip; and the many volunteers who took time to walk and describe each of the walks contained in this book.
To St John Ambulance Australia for First Aid information.
To Bob Cooper Outdoor Education for bushcraft and safety information.
Thank you all for your support in this project.

© 1993. ISBN 0-7309-6108-7
Reprint © 2005. ISBN 0-7307-5505-3

DEPARTMENT OF
Conservation
AND LAND MANAGEMENT
Conserving the nature of WA

CONTENTS

THE SOUTH WALKS 37 - 48   135

INDEX BY WALK LENGTH   163

CALM OFFICES   165

YANCHEP NATIONAL PARK.

Introduction

ABOUT THIS BOOK

Family Walks in Perth Outdoors is designed to complement the Department of Conservation and Land Management's best selling book *Perth Outdoors: A Guide to Natural Recreation Areas in and around Perth*.

The 50 walks described in this book are listed first by geographical location (Hills, North, River and South) and then alphabetically by name within those regions. Each walk is numbered. There is also an index by walk length at the back of the book.

Each walk has a mud map and a description of some of the things you might see along the way. The majority of walks have carparks and picnic facilities at the start or nearby. Some have toilets, water and other facilities.

Distances and travelling times from Perth GPO are approximate and walk times are based on taking a leisurely stroll rather than a brisk walk.

The walk classes, based on Australian Standards walktrack classifications, are given as a guide for you to use to judge your ability to undertake the walk. They are as follows:

• Class 1 – Walks that cater for a range of visitors, including those with reduced mobility and people who are wheelchair assisted. Walktrails are generally well marked and broad, with hardened surfaces. They usually include interpretation and other facilities. No experience is required. Users are expected to exercise normal care regarding their personal safety.

• Class 2 – Walks that cater for a range of visitors. Walktrails are generally well marked, have hardened surfaces, and may have steps. They usually include interpretation and other facilities. No experience is required. Users are expected to exercise normal care regarding their personal safety.

• Class 3 – Users require a moderate level of fitness. Trails may be slightly modified, and include a combination of steps, some hardened sections and unstable surfaces. They can include limited interpretation and facilities. Weather can affect safety.

• Class 4 – Distinct tracks in relatively undisturbed natural environments. Trails are often rough and have few, if any, modifications. A moderate to high level of fitness is required. Users need to be self-reliant. There may be few encounters with others. Weather can affect safety.

• Class 5 – Mostly indistinct trails through undisturbed natural environments. Terrain is rough. A high level of fitness is required. Users must be prepared and self reliant, with advanced outdoor knowledge. There are few encounters with others. Weather can affect safety.

While every effort has been made to ensure that the information provided in this book is accurate, no responsibility can be taken for any changes made since the walks were surveyed, or for the state of repair of any walk, as this is subject to weather and usage. When walking in the bush or along established trails, it is important to tread carefully and keep your eyes open for potential hazards.

Your safety is our concern, but your responsibility.

WALKING IN PERTH OUTDOORS

Walking through natural bushland is a pleasurable experience. To be surrounded by the sounds, colours, smells and different types of life forms in and around Perth is both enlightening and exhilarating. Few capital cities are blessed with such a variety of natural areas right on their doorstep.

The natural environment of Perth is made up of four distinctive natural communities, or ecosystems:

- the forests and woodlands of the Darling Range and Scarp;
- the woodlands of the coastal plain;
- the wetlands that fringe lakes, streams, rivers and estuaries; and
- the coastal and marine environments.

These distinctive natural communities are characterised by the soil type, landform and dominant plant life. The plants, animals, insects and other invertebrates, micro-organisms, rocks, soil, water, aspect to the sun and resultant microclimate all combine in subtle ways within each community to make each walk different. Wherever you choose to walk within a natural community you can see both the common and specific characteristics that make each place special.

The forests and woodlands of the Darling Range and Scarp

The Darling Range is the tilted edge of a huge plateau that is the foundation of this part of Western Australia. Here, some of the oldest rocks on Earth are exposed. The granites, gneisses and quartzites are more than 2500 million years old.

The overlying mantle of reddish-orange laterite rock formed about 10 million years ago, when wetter and more humid conditions than those of today leached minerals from the soil to form a hard, insoluble crust. Jarrah trees, with their stringy greyish-black bark, are predominant. Jarrah forest, with its low understorey of wildflowers and groves of grasstrees, is an integral defining image of the Darling Range, particularly when backlit by the sun in the early morning and late afternoon.

The western extremity of the Darling Range is the Darling Scarp. Standing 200 metres or so above the coastal plain, it is the distinctive feature of the Perth horizon. The scarp exposes huge granite rocks and favours white-trunked wandoo trees.

The woodlands of the coastal plain

The forested foothills below the Darling Scarp spill onto the coastal plain. Here, the less fertile sands support woodlands of banksia, sheoaks, stunted eucalypts of jarrah and marri, and, where creamy grey limestone is exposed, groves of tuart and pricklybark. Shrublands and wildflower heathlands form the understorey. In the wetter areas, paperbarks proliferate. In late winter and spring, the trees, shrubs and heathlands display their presence with a profusion of flowers.

A complex of sand dune systems is aligned roughly parallel to the coast. These were formed during the past two million years from wind-blown beach sand deposits along previous shorelines of this coastal plain.

The coastal woodlands are a distinctively different community to that of the forests of the range. Compare the rocks and gravels of the range with the sands of the plain; the tall trees of the forest with the shorter-trunked, deep-crowned woodland trees and shrublands on the plain.

The wetlands fringing lakes, rivers, streams and estuaries

The apparent uniformity of the coastal woodlands is broken by urban developments and the wetlands of the coastal plain, which include the Swan and Canning rivers and the chains of lakes to the north and south of the Swan.

The presence of wetlands is indicated by paperbark woodland, which is tolerant of wet conditions. The combination of smooth-barked, graceful flooded gums and densely-foliaged, twisting-trunked paperbarks fringing cool waterbodies creates pleasant and tranquil walking experiences.

The many freshwater lakes, dotted throughout the coastal plain, appear like scattered jewels from vantage points through surrounding woodlands of banksia and paperbarks. These wetlands provide habitat for waders and other waterbirds and a myriad of other creatures, such as frogs and turtles, that rely on damp conditions to survive the long, dry summers.

The coastal and marine environments

Rocky limestone outcrops and sweeping white sand dunes along the Perth coast, with a plant cover of wattles and other shrubs, abut the bluish-green waters of the Indian Ocean. Beneath the waves there is a seascape of limestone ledges, walls, caves, reefs and islands that provide habitat for a wonderful diversity of marine life.

WALKING SAFELY

This book is designed for people looking for enjoyable walks along existing tracks through parks, reserves or along riverbanks, in mostly natural areas such as forests, woodlands or coastal areas.

However, all natural areas have a degree of danger; for example, slippery or uneven surfaces. Walking along tracks, trails and firebreaks is relatively safe, but you should still be alert to potential hazards. Most of the information in this section is common sense, but additional safety and first aid information have been included in the unlikely event of someone in your party being injured or getting lost.

Be prepared:

- Wear sturdy but comfortable footwear. Training shoes may be suitable, but care should be taken when crossing uneven or slippery surfaces like damp or mossy rocks. In these cases, it is desirable to wear boots that give some support to the ankles. Always wear good quality, fairly thick, cotton or wool socks.
- Long socks or long trousers will protect legs against prickly vegetation or biting insects. A long-sleeved shirt will help to protect you from sunburn in summer and a woollen sweater or fleece top will help to keep you warm in winter. It is best to dress in layers of light clothing that can be peeled on or off as required.
- Take a light raincoat.
- Wear a hat for protection against the sun or rain.
- Use sunscreen with a minimum sun protection factor (SPF) of 15+.
- Carry gear in a light day pack, to keep your hands free.
- If you are making an extended or difficult walk, tell at least two people your exact plans and advise them when you've completed the walk.
- Take a first aid kit and insect repellent.
- Walk in a party of two or more people for safety. If you are injured, you will need someone who can summon help.
- Make sure you have at least two litres of water per person on most days, and at least three litres on hot days.

If you become lost:

- Try to retrace your steps until you reach a recognisable place on the map.
- If you cannot retrace your steps, follow a track; it will usually lead to some habitation. Alternatively, head for the nearest high point and climb to the summit. You will then be able to see roads and areas of habitation.
- If you are still lost and have run out of water, remember that animal trails are likely to lead to water. Walk in the direction in which the trails converge into one. Watch out for flocks of birds; they fly rapidly towards water and more slowly when travelling away from water after drinking.

FIRST AID

Carry a first aid kit with the following basic essentials:
- Antiseptic cream and swabs
- Aspirin or Paracetamol
- Band aids
- Dressings (sterile)
- Gloves
- Scissors
- Snake bite bandage
- Triangular bandage
- Tweezers

Snake bites

Although several species of snake inhabit the areas dealt with in this book, it is very unlikely that you will see one, let alone be bitten by one. Snakes sense the vibration of approaching footsteps and tend to flee into the undergrowth. If you *are* unlucky enough to be bitten, assume the snake is poisonous and take the following action:

DO NOT panic: Try to remain calm, lie down and immobilise the bitten area.

DO NOT wash the wound: Venom left on the skin will help doctors identify the snake so that they can administer the appropriate anti-venene.

DO NOT apply a tourniquet: Take out the snake bandage and bind, not too tightly, along the limb starting at the bite area, then bandage down the limb and continue back up above the bite area. This will help to prevent the spread of the venom through the body. Do not remove the bandage.

DO NOT elevate the limb or attempt to walk or run: Movement will encourage the spread of the venom through the body. If necessary, immobilise the limb with a splint. Lie down and keep still until help arrives.

DO NOT attempt to catch the snake: Two bitten people will be more difficult to deal with than one, and if there are only two of you, you'll need someone who can go for help.

Sprains and broken limbs

Although most of the walks in this book are along existing, well-walked trails, some have uneven or loose surfaces along the route. Where possible, these have been indicated in the text, but you should always tread carefully as areas can become loose or uneven after heavy rain or very dry periods. If you or a fellow walker trips and sprains or breaks a limb, you should take the following action.

With sprains apply the 'RICE' technique:

R- REST and reassure the casualty.
I - ICE: Apply an ice pack, or cloth soaked in cold water, for 15-20 minutes. It may be reapplied every two hours for the first 24 hours.
C- COMPRESSION: Bandage the sprain firmly.
E- ELEVATE the sprained limb and support the injury.

Remember to avoid both heat and massage.

If the limb is broken and the casualty is conscious and breathing freely, take the following action:

DO control any bleeding.
DO rest and reassure the casualty.
DO immobilise the fractured limb with splints and slings in the most comfortable position and check the blood circulation past the last bandaging point. Be sure to handle the casualty carefully.
DO NOT pull on any fractures.
DO NOT give the casualty anything to drink.
DO NOT force or straighten fractured joints.

The first aid information provided here is very basic. St John Ambulance Australia publishes first aid manuals, sells first aid kits and runs a variety of first aid courses. For more information contact your nearest St John Ambulance Centre, call (08) 9334 1233 or visit their website (www.ambulance.net.au).

AUSTRALIAN ADMIRAL

WHAT YOU NEED TO KNOW

Bushwalking

You can bushwalk either by using walking tracks or by trekking through wild bush. While the first is usually safe and relaxing, the second may do environmental damage and put your life at risk, especially if you are not well prepared.

The walks in this book follow either formalised walktrails with signs and occasionally surfaced tracks, or well used and informally established tracks through bushland, parks or riverside areas. Some of the walks cross or form part of the Bibbulmun Track. This is a 965-kilometre, long-distance walk track from Kalamunda, in the Darling Range east of Perth, to Albany, on the South Coast.

Camping

While out walking you may see possible sites for a future camping expedition. In order to protect our environment and drinking water catchments, visitors may only camp at designated camping sites – usually marked with a sign in national parks, regional parks, State forest or bush areas. Please leave no rubbish or other traces of your visit. Camping fees are charged in some areas and the funds raised help to pay for the facilities and services provided.

Dieback

Some areas of forest and woodland have been infected by a soil-borne pathogen (*Phytophthora cinnamomi*) that attacks the root systems of trees, shrubs and wildflowers. The disease is known to attack at least 900 plant species and many, such as banksias and dryandras, die very quickly. The pathogen travels over and through the soil in water, attaching to roots. The rot sets in immediately.

The pathogen that causes dieback is carried in soil or mud that sticks to boots and shoes, and the wheels, mudguards and underbodies of vehicles, including mountain bikes. When the soil or mud drops off, the pathogen immediately contaminates the new area and multiplies. There is, as yet, no known broad-scale cure.

Some areas in national parks and State forest are closed to vehicles to prevent dieback being carried into or spread through them. These areas are largely uninfected. You may enter on foot but you must not take vehicles, motorbikes, horses or any form of wheeled transport into these areas. When walking through infected areas, help stop the rot by not straying from the track. Observe the signs and give our plants a chance.

Entry fees ($)

Entry fees are charged for vehicle entry in to some parks and reserves. Where a charge is made, it is indicated in this book by the symbol ($). The funds raised help to pay for the facilities and services provided.

Fire

Bushfires are a real danger, particularly during the dry summer months. Avoid extended walks in the Perth hills at this time.

- Only use the fireplaces provided. Better still, bring your own portable stove.
- Open fires are not permitted in national parks.
- No fires are permitted anywhere on days of high or extreme fire danger and in the Perth hills between November and April.
- Clear all leaf litter, dead branches and anything else that may burn from an area of at least three metres around and above the fire. This also applies to portable stoves.
- Never leave a fire unattended.
- Make sure the fire is completely out before leaving. Use soil and water to extinguish the embers, and bury the ashes.

On certain days during the year the fire forecast is 'very high' or 'extreme'. A total fire ban exists on these days. Local radio stations broadcast fire risk warnings, but please check with local authorities, the tourist bureau, or the nearest Department of Conservation and Land Management (CALM) office for advice on the fire situation.

Firearms

No offensive weapon is to be brought into any conservation or recreation area.

Fishing

Fisheries regulations apply in all areas, but you should also check with the ranger in any national park. Trout and redfin perch have been stocked in inland waters near Perth. Marron fishing is a seasonal activity by permit only. We'd like you to come back, so help to conserve fish numbers by complying with bag limits set by the Department of Fisheries and by taking only enough for your immediate needs.

Granite outcrops

Several walks in this book cross or pass close to granite outcrops. Granite outcrops, often termed 'living rocks', are unique sanctuaries for many species of plants and animals. Exploring granite outcrops is a fascinating experience, but the

14

environment is extremely fragile. Moving a rock, disturbing a plant or carelessly placing a foot can cause irreparable damage. Granite outcrops throughout the South West are often also sites of great cultural significance for Nyoongar people. Please do not stray off the tracks that cross granite outcrops, do not move any rocks or create or add to existing rock cairns and do be careful where you place your feet.

Native plants and animals

In order to protect the environment, please do not disturb any native animals, and do not pick the wildflowers. Rocks, vegetation or old logs should not be removed as these are often the homes of small creatures that depend on such habitats.

Pets, Western Shield and 1080 baiting

Unless there is a specially designated dog area, you are usually not allowed to take your pet into national and conservation parks, nature reserves and water catchments. Many other parks and reserves managed by local authorities have similar restrictions. If you are not sure whether dogs and/or other pets are permitted at the place you intend to visit, please leave them at home. Visually impaired people with guide dogs can take their dogs into any CALM-managed area.

CALM is currently undertaking *Western Shield*, the world's biggest campaign against feral predators. Foxes and cats have already contributed to the extinction of 10 native mammal species, and threaten many others. *Western Shield* aims to reduce feral cat and fox populations through baiting programs using 1080, a poison that occurs naturally in WA and does not harm native wildlife.

However, dogs and cats are very susceptible to 1080 poisoning, for which there is no antidote. Warning signs are placed prominently around baited areas, so visitors know there are baits around. Domestic dogs and cats should not be allowed to roam in areas that have been baited, so to ensure their safety please leave them at home.

Rubbish

Place all litter in bins provided. If there are no bins, take your litter home with you. When camping or walking in the bush, bury organic waste at least 15 centimetres deep and at least 100 metres from any waterway, picnic area or campsite.

Vehicles

Normal road rules apply in all recreation and conservation areas. To protect wildlife habitat and the environment from erosion and dieback disease, please keep to formed roads and designated tracks at all times. Be sure to lock your vehicle if it is left unattended.

Water

Most creeks and rivers in Western Australia are dry during the summer months. When you are out and about take your own drinking water. If you do have to use water from the few permanent water points, it should be boiled before use, or purified using a commercially available purification product.

Water catchments

These special areas are reserved for water and vegetation protection. Because of this, there are restrictions on various recreation activities in certain areas. Check with the WA Water Authority.

Leave no trace

- **Plan ahead and prepare:** Prepare for extreme weather, hazards and emergencies. Walk in small groups. Take maps and a compass and know how to use them.
- **Walk and camp on durable surfaces:** Always walk on the track – even when wet or muddy – and walk just wide of the centre to avoid compaction and erosion, especially in sandy coastal areas.
- **Dispose of waste properly:** Carry out all rubbish and leftover food. Deposit solid human waste in holes dug 15-25 centimetres deep, at least 100 metres from water, camps and tracks. Cover and disguise the hole when finished. To wash yourself or your dishes, carry water 100 metres from streams or lakes and use only small amounts of biodegradable soap.
- **Leave what you find:** Respect indigenous art and other sites of cultural significance. Preserve the past: examine, but do not touch cultural or historic structures and artefacts. Leave rocks, plants and other natural objects as you find them. Avoid introducing or transporting non-native species such as weeds.
- **Minimise campfires and their impacts:** Where fires are permitted, only use designated constructed fireplaces. Keep fires small. Only use dead, fallen fuel and sticks from the ground that can be broken by hand. Burn all wood and coals to ash, and put out the fire completely before leaving. Take notice of all fire weather forecasts.
- **Respect wildlife and plant life:** Observe wildlife from a distance. Do not follow or approach them. Never feed animals, which damages their health and alters natural protective behaviours. Avoid spread of soil-borne plant diseases by keeping boots free of soil when walking through disease risk areas, and using only approved vehicle access points. Pets are not permitted in national parks and in some other areas. Check before you bring your dog or cat. Control pets at all times or leave them at home.
- **Be considerate of your hosts and other users:** Respect other walkers and protect the quality of their experience. Be courteous. Give way to other users on the walktrail. Let nature's sounds prevail. Avoid loud voices and noises.

The Hills   Walks 1 – 10

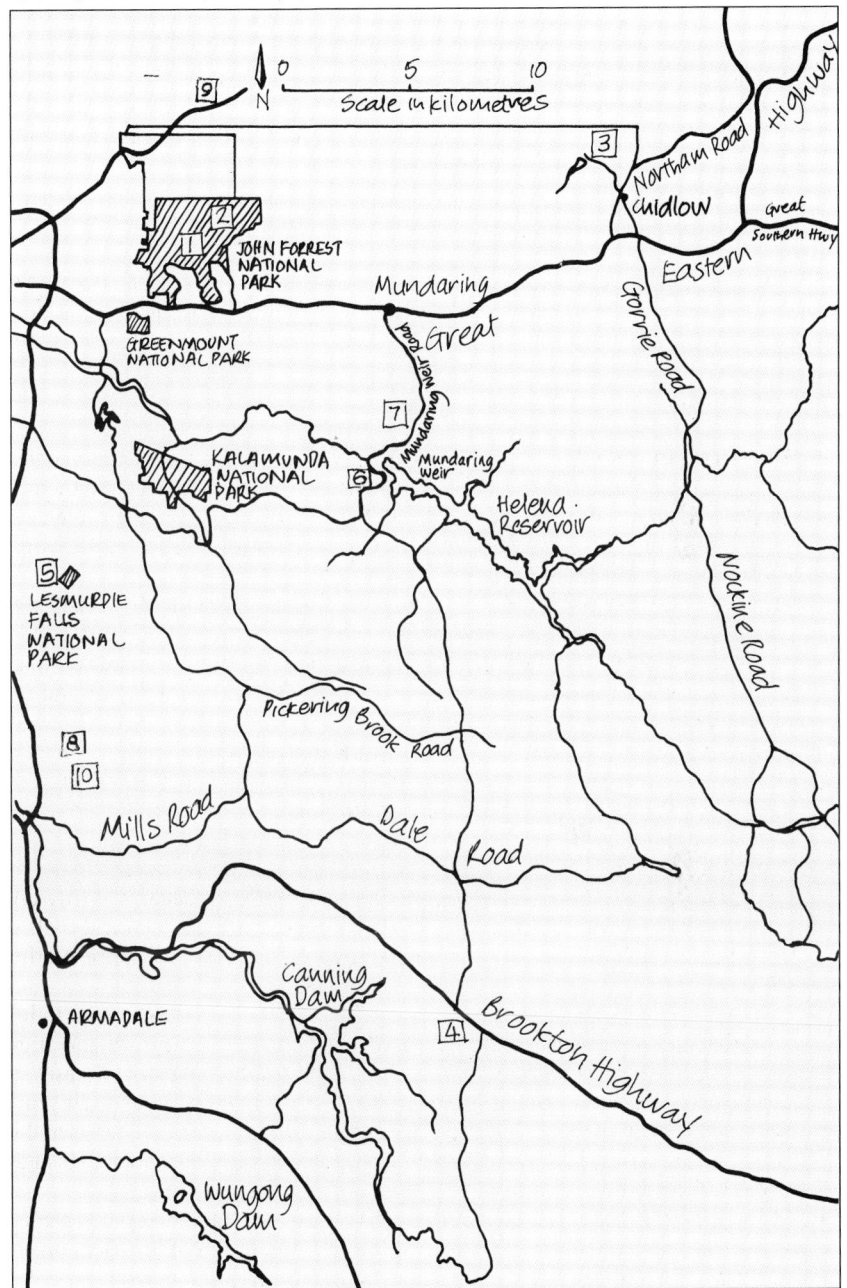

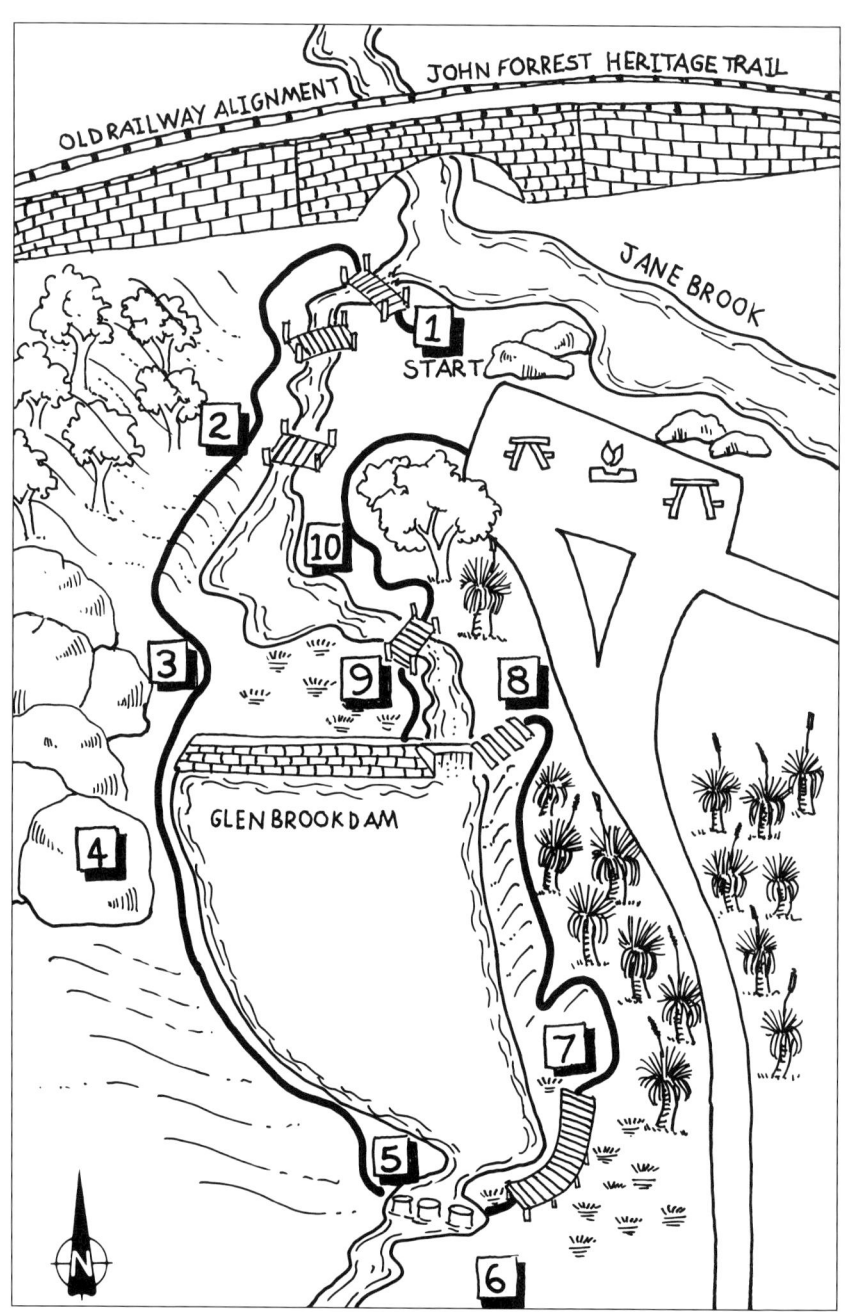

Glen Brook Trail

John Forrest National Park ($)

Length: *2.2 km loop.*
Class: *3.*
Walk time: *45 minutes.*

This walk starts and finishes at the main picnic area in John Forrest National Park and skirts the Glen Brook Dam. It features scenic views over the dam and a multitude of wildflowers during spring.

1   Leave from the north-western corner of the picnic area and cross a footbridge over Glen Brook where it converges with Jane Brook. Turn left after crossing the bridge and head along the brook side.
2   An old 1930s-style picnic shelter, nestled below the steep hillside covered in woodland of wandoo, marri and jarrah, overlooks the current picnic area on the opposite side of the brook. Small bridges cross the brook. From here, the track rises slowly towards the dam.
3   The Glen Brook Dam was built in the 1960s to provide additional water supplies for the park. Follow the trail around the dam.
4   A large granite outcrop on the right of the trail is set back among the trees on the slope.
5   Cross over Glen Brook at the southern end of the dam using stepping posts. The brook flows only in winter.
6   Head north again on the boardwalk over a swampy area.
7   The trail climbs over a small ridge from which there are elevated views of the dam. Grasstrees dominate the slopes on this side.
8   On reaching the dam wall, step down onto the wall and cross the spillway.
9   Descend more steps and rejoin the trail below. Cross the footbridge over the spillway.
10 The trail follows the line of the brook back to the picnic area.

David Briggs, Karl Mucjanko

Where is it? *26 km east of Perth in John Forrest National Park.*
Travelling time: *40 minutes from Perth via Great Eastern Highway.*
Facilities: *BBQs, kiosk, tavern, tables, water, toilets, carpark.*
On-site information: *Trailhead sign, directional signs along the route.*
Best season: *All year, spring for wildflowers.*

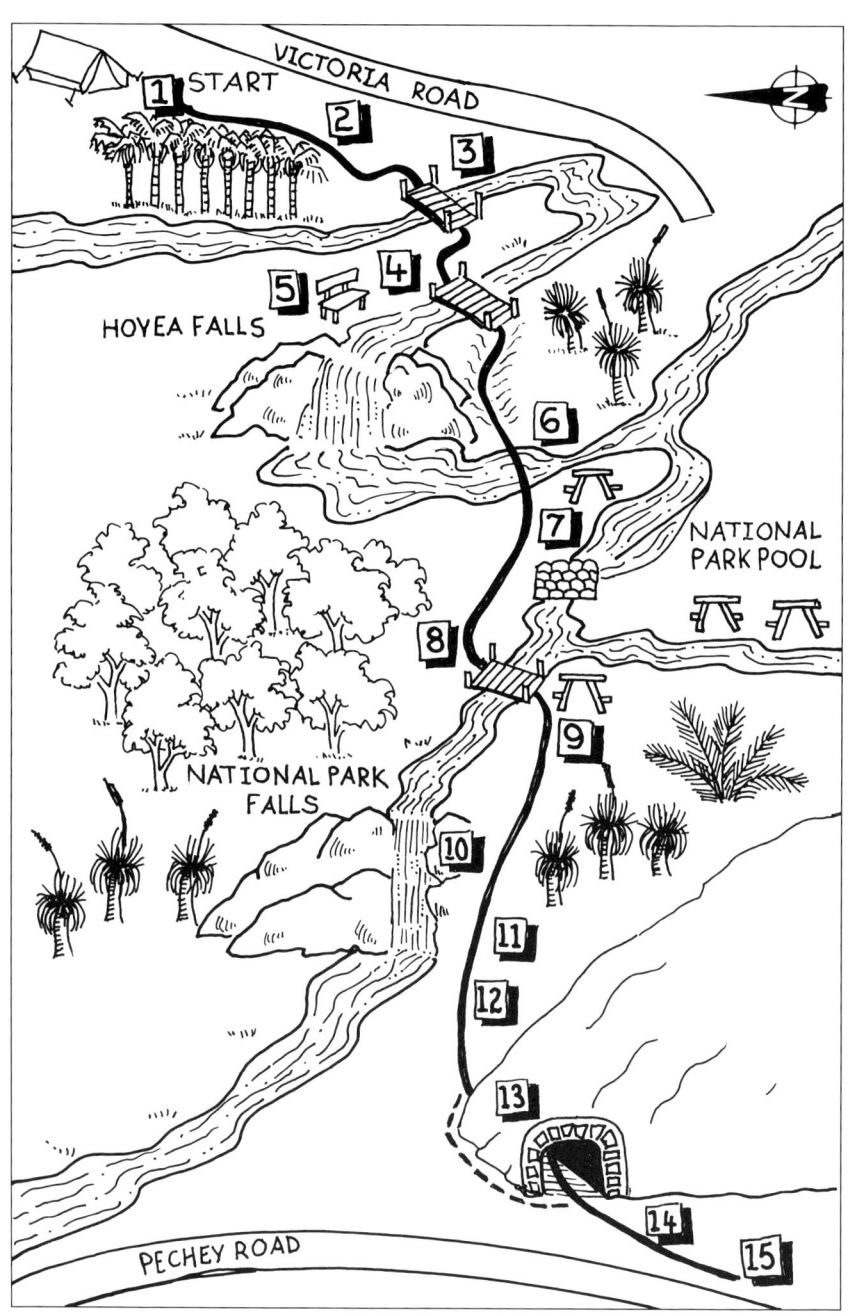

John Forrest Heritage Trail   **2**

John Forrest National Park ($)

Length: *10.2 km return.*
Class: *3.*
Walk time: *2 hours, 15 minutes.*

This walk runs along the route of the old Eastern Railway line, which passed through the national park. It is a long, sloping walk from east to west with ballast underfoot. The walk can be taken from either Pechey Road or Victoria Road, or partway from the main picnic area near the old National Park Station.

1   Hovea Station campsite.
2   Eight large palms mark the site of Hovea Station. The station was the first siding where visitors could alight from the train. A crossing loop was built in 1912 as a place for loading timber.
3   A pair of old railway bridges for two-way traffic lie about 600 metres from Hovea Station.
4   A second pair of bridges is a further 200 metres along the trail.
5   Hovea Falls is named after the holly-leaf hovea (*Hovea chorizemifolia*), which, when in season, can be seen in the vicinity.
6   Deep Creek Bridge. Although it is now filled beneath, the original bridge remains and you can still see the timbers. At 125.7 metres, this was the longest trestle bridge constructed on this line.
7   The main picnic area is adjacent to the Jane Brook, below the walkway. The steps, garden walls and footpaths were constructed by sustenance workers during the Great Depression of the 1930s.
8   Jane Brook Bridge was built on this site in 1895. By the 1920s, it had deteriorated and gravel was used to reinforce it. In 1928, the structure was changed to steel and concrete to cater for heavier loads.
9   The foundations seen here are all that remains of the National Park Station, which was built for park visitors in 1936 as an alternative stop to Hovea Station.
10 National Park Falls. Jane Brook drops some 25 metres over massive granite rocks, which outcrop from the ancient bedrock of the Darling Scarp. The falls are at their best during and after winter rains between July and September.
11 On 30 June 1896, a goods and passenger train bound for Northam set down passengers at Lion Mill, 13.5 kilometres up the line from here. A coupling broke soon afterwards and 22 of its 24 carriages started rolling towards Perth. They crashed here at 193 kph, killing eight horses and one person.

12 At this point there are excellent views across the valley to the Swan Coastal Plain.
13 Old Railway Tunnel. This tunnel, completed in 1895, is 240 metres long and is the only major railway tunnel in WA. You may walk through the tunnel or skirt around the outside.
14 This is the site of the main campsite that housed the railway construction team in tents.
15 The end of the walk at Pechey Road. Arrange to be collected here or return along the same route to Victoria Road.

Karl Mucjanko and Mark Moore

Where is it? *26 km east of Perth in John Forrest National Park. The trail starts from Victoria Road, Hovea.*
Travelling time: *40 minutes from Perth via Great Eastern Highway and Brooking Road.*
Facilities: *BBQs, kiosk, tavern, tables, water, toilets, carpark.*
On-site information: *Trailhead signs (both ends), interpretive plaques along the route.*
Best season: *Autumn, winter for falls, spring for wildflowers.*

BALGAS (GRASSTREES)

One of the commonest plants in our local bush is the balga, a type of grasstree.

Around Perth, five different species of grasstree occur; some have no trunk, some a very spiky flower and another has comparatively small clumps of foliage and a slender flower spike.

Grasstrees only grow in Australia and there are 28 species altogether, nine of which occur in WA. They were a tremendous resource for Aboriginal people. They provided food, material for building shelters and material to make tools for fire lighting.

Possibly the best known and most easily recognised species in the Perth metropolitan area is the *Xanthorrhoea preissii*, called balga by the local Nyoongar people. This species develops a tall, sometimes twisted trunk and is the only one to grow more than three metres high.

In spring, balga produces an impressive spear or flower spike, up to four metres long and six centimetres thick. Thousands of buds are tightly packed on the top two thirds of the spear and open into tiny white flowers in mid to late spring. After flowering, the spear produces beak-like capsules, which release shiny black seeds in summer and autumn.

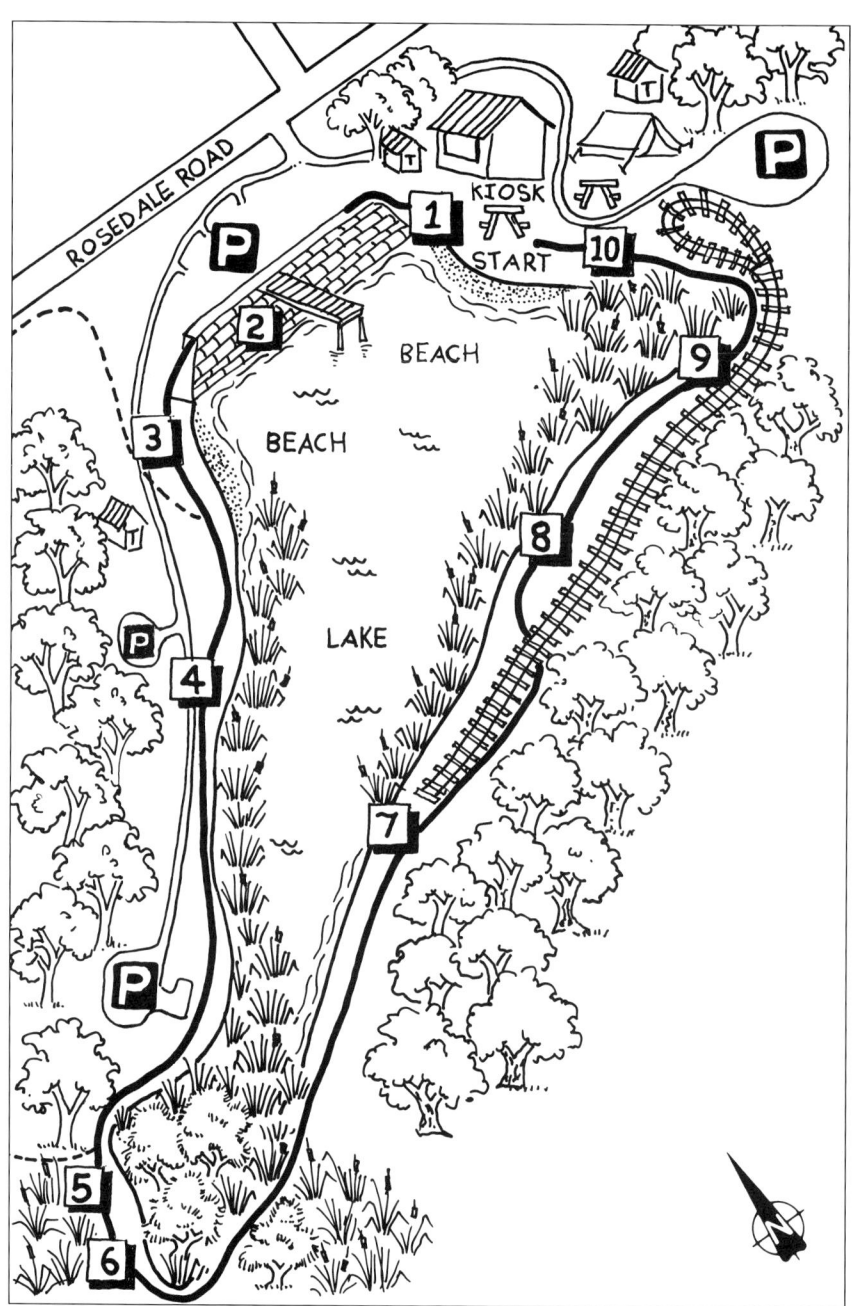

Lakeside Walktrail

Lake Leschenaultia ($)

3

Length: *3 km loop.*
Class: *2.*
Walk time: *1 hour.*

This is a very pleasant walk around the lake, especially after a barbecue lunch. For the more adventurous, there is a longer (six kilometre) walk that takes you through the jarrah forest to the west of the lake.

Note: Dogs are not permitted in the park.

1 Start at the eastern end of the dam wall adjacent to the main picnic area.
2 Midway along the wall is a diving platform. Swimming in the lake is popular in summer. Leave the dam wall, turn left and follow the track along the beach front.
3 The alternative six kilometre walktrail branches off at this point.
4 Along this section there are woodlands of jarrah and marri on the slopes to the right and reeds around the lake's edge.
5 The reeds become more prominent at the south-western corner of the lake. Here, the longer trail rejoins.
6 As you turn at the far end of the lake, paperbarks are found in wet areas on each side of the track.
7 Head back up along the eastern side of the lake until you come to the terminus of the miniature railway.
8 Wandoos dominate the vegetation beyond the railway track.
9 At the eastern corner of the lake there are more reeds and coojong or golden wreath wattle (*Acacia saligna*).
10 Continue past the railway station and across lawns to the main picnic area.

Alan Hill

Where is it? *40 km east of Perth, north of Chidlow.*
Travelling time: *1 hour from Perth via Great Eastern Highway.*
Facilities: *BBQs, picnic sites, water, toilets, carparks, kiosk.*
On-site information: *Occasional trail markers.*
Best season: *All year.*

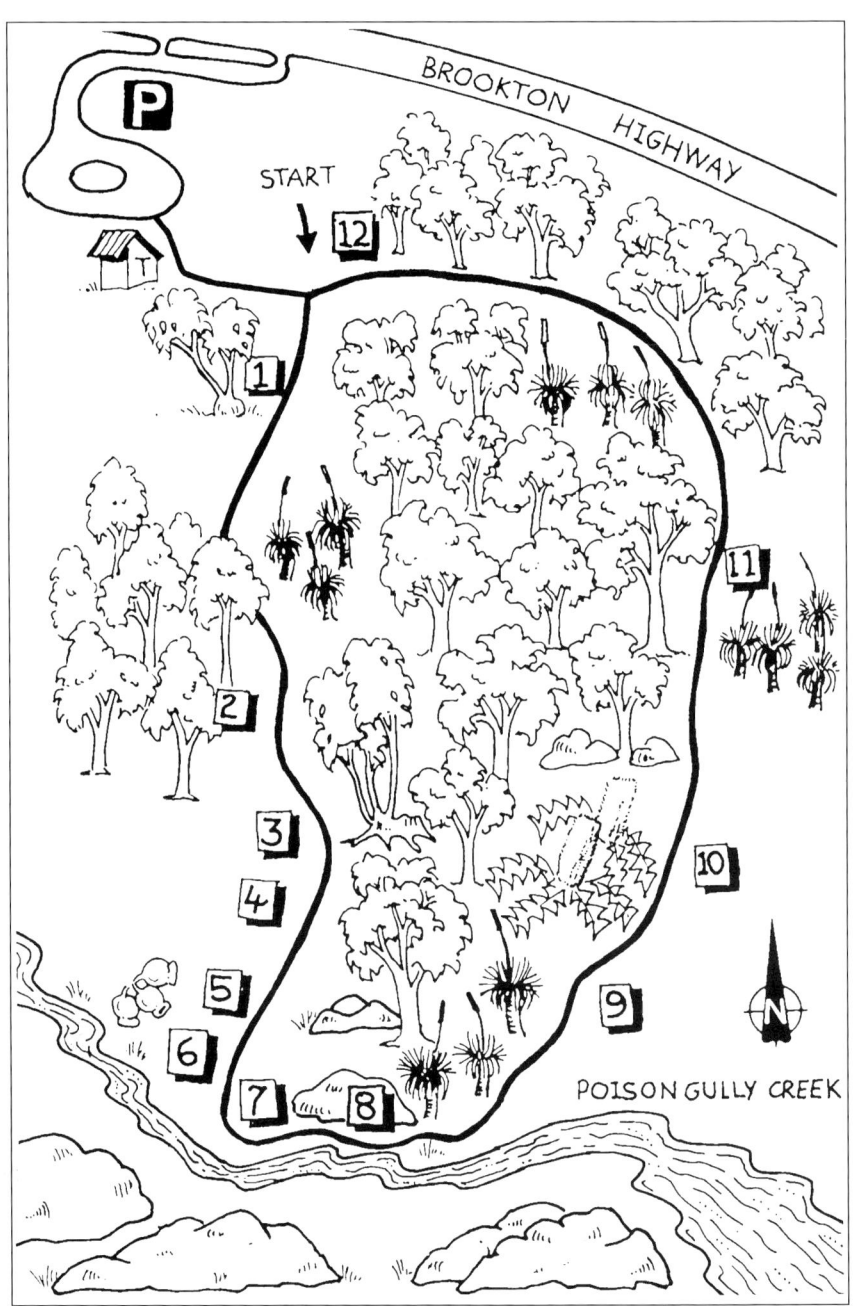

Lesley Nature Trail   **4**

Length: *1.5 km loop.*
Class: *4.*
Walk time: *45 minutes.*

The forest is a complex biological community of living organisms that is continually changing. This trail takes you through the forest life cycle and features forestry techniques and tree species of the northern jarrah forest.

1 Starting from the picnic area, head in a southerly direction past the toilet. The track winds its way through the jarrah forest for approximately 180 metres before hitting a firebreak. At this firebreak turn left and then, after about five metres, turn right. Keep following this track, as it is a loop trail, and will eventually bring you back to this point.

2 In its first year, jarrah (*Eucalyptus marginata*) produces a small lignotuber at the base of its stem. This is an organ of food storage and regeneration, and contains a store of living buds. Small shoots will emerge and, as the lignotuber becomes larger, the plant will produce a single vigorous stem, which eventually becomes the trunk of a new tree. Once the single shoot has emerged, the young jarrah tree will continue to grow into a pole, unless damaged by insect attack, fire or frost. Jarrah is characterised by grey stringy bark and a straight trunk, which can reach a height of 20 metres and a diameter of two metres.

3 Many eucalypts, including jarrah, may regenerate by coppice shoots from a stump. These form when a mature tree is damaged by wind or storm, or when it is cut down.

4 Not all trees, even those of the same species, develop into a form that will be useful for timber. Some may develop large, heavy limbs and crooked trunks, while others may have been damaged by intense wildfire or insect attack.

5 Some trees are removed to make way for young regrowth. Others are retained as food and shelter for wildlife, and to stabilise the soil. An old method used to kill a tree was ringbarking. A strip of the outer living wood of the trunk (which transports water and nutrients) was removed and the tree eventually died.

6 Another common tree of the jarrah forest is marri (*Corymbia calophylla*). This tree is easily recognised by its large gumnuts and the red gum seen oozing from its trunk. This is caused by insects boring into the heartwood and releasing the characteristic red sap.

7   The track heads roughly eastwards, parallel to Poison Gully Creek for a short time. A shrub called York Road poison (*Gastrolobium calycinum*) grows in this valley and is toxic all year round, hence the gully's name.

8   As the trail meanders along the stream you will see a decline in the number of trees, while the scrub becomes thicker. Here, the soil may be very shallow or non-existent, and large areas of exposed rock appear. Although trees find it difficult to survive in this environment, other plants, such as grasstrees (*Xanthorrhoea preissii*), have adapted and thrive. Thicker creek vegetation is a particularly good habitat for most forest animals.

9   Apart from jarrah and marri, several other tree species are found in the Perth Outdoors area. Blackbutt (*Eucalyptus patens*), also called yarri, grows in moist areas along creeks and rivers. Although it is similar to jarrah, blackbutt can be recognised by its drooping bluish-green leaves, which are longer and narrower than those of jarrah, and the fibrous, deeply fissured bark of mature trees. Along the trail you will walk through a buttress of large blackbutts.

10 Another tree found in the understorey of the jarrah forest is the bull banksia (*Banksia grandis*), distinguishable by its large serrated leaves. Its yellow, candle-shaped flowers, large woody cone and gnarled growth habit make it an attractive species. It is one of several plants that are very susceptible to dieback, caused by the soil-borne root-rot pathogen *Phytophthora cinnamomi*.

11 This tree was left during a logging operation in 1950, to provide a seed source for regeneration. The small trees you can see surrounding this large one are the results of this modern forest management technique, which ensures that for every jarrah tree removed there will be at least one young seedling ready to take its place.

12 After 1550 metres, the trail arrives back at the firebreak where you turned left at point 1. To get back to the picnic area turn left onto the firebreak, and then turn right after about 15 metres. This track will take you back to the picnic area via the toilet.

Peter Gibson, Jamie Ridley, Michael Phillips

Where is it? *47 km from Perth and about 20 km from Kelmscott along Brookton Highway.*
Travelling time: *1 hour from Perth.*
Facilities: *BBQs, toilet, picnic tables.*
Best season: *Spring for wildflowers.*

BRUSHTAIL POSSUMS

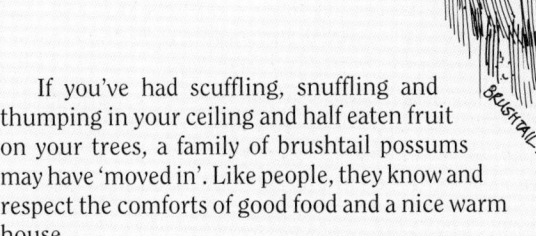

If you've had scuffling, snuffling and thumping in your ceiling and half eaten fruit on your trees, a family of brushtail possums may have 'moved in'. Like people, they know and respect the comforts of good food and a nice warm house.

Brushtail possums (*Trichosurus vulpecula*) are normally found in open forests and woodlands, where they nest high up in tree hollows, although they also spend considerable amounts of time on the ground. They often occupy the same tree for years, or even generations.

Male brushtail possums are territorial. Females seem to be more flexible and will occasionally share territories with other females, or move in and share a male's home tree when nesting.

After the young are born and weaned, they move out to seek their own trees and territories some distance from their mother's home range.

The main requirement of any brushtail possum is a suitably sized hollow high enough above the ground. Because large cavities in trees are usually formed by broken branches, possum trees tend to be large, old, in decline or dead. You can usually tell a possum tree by the pathway of scratch marks that leads up the trunk and, sometimes, droppings at the base of the tree.

Brushtail possums are nocturnal so you will be lucky to see one during the day.

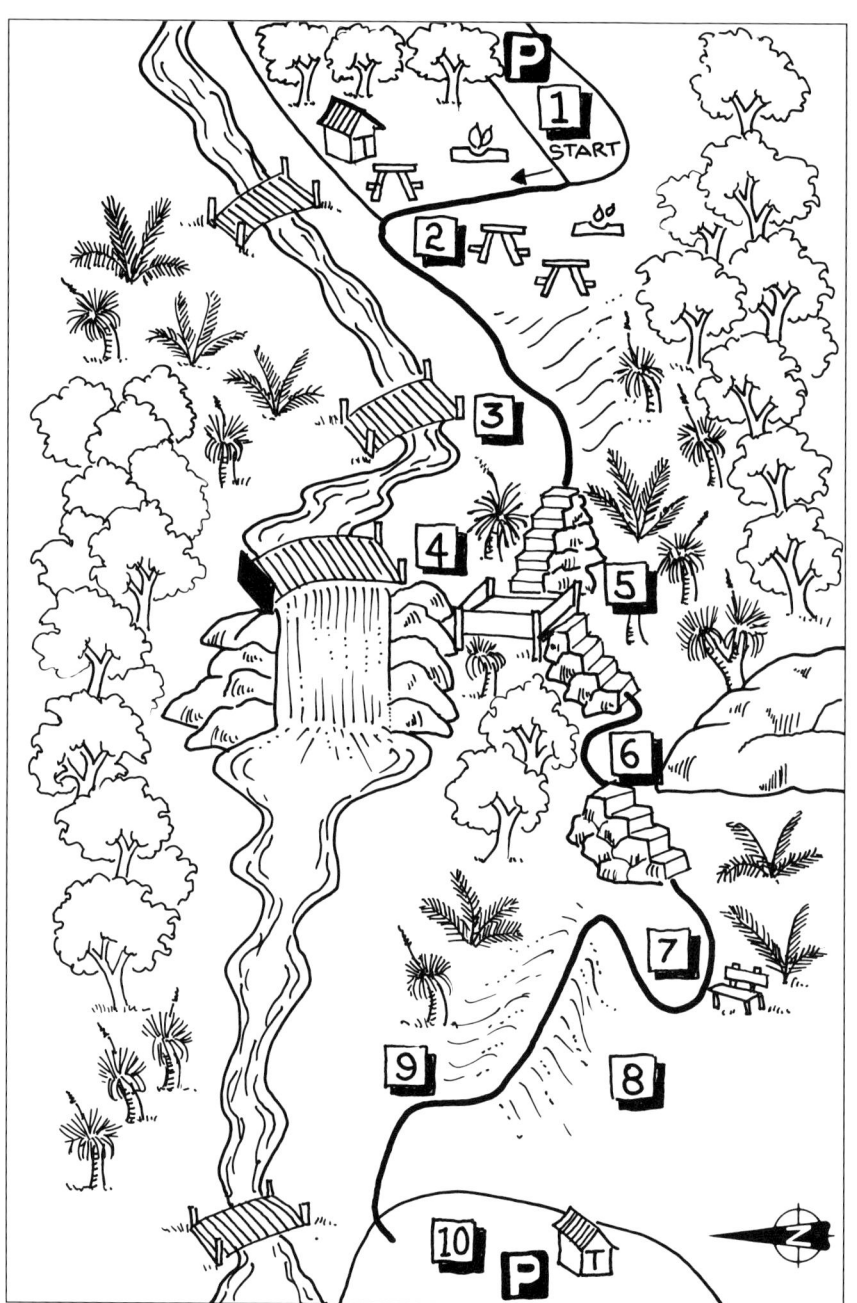

Lesmurdie Falls Walktrail   **5**

Lesmurdie Falls National Park

Length: *2 km return.*
Class: *4.*
Walk time: *1 hour, 30 minutes.*

The main feature of this walk is the falls, and there is a viewing platform that provides views both up and down the valley. For the most part, the trail runs gradually downhill on the side of the valley, before descending more steeply to the edge of the brook near the end. Allow ample time to return along the track, which climbs constantly until you reach the top of the falls. There are several bird species in the area, including kestrels, and the sounds of frogs can be heard after winter rains. This walk is particularly rewarding in early spring, when the park is ablaze with wildflowers and the brook is still flowing strongly over the falls.

1   Walking down from the western end of the carpark, you pass through a pleasant picnic area with barbecues and ample tables. The trail continues down a slight slope.
2   When you reach the small bridge over the brook, do not cross it, but turn left along the blue metal track by the side of the brook. This part of the trail features marris, rushes and sedges by the water's edge and granite outcrops on your left. Another track joins from the left and a second bridge crosses the brook.
3   As you move upwards, you will gain views out over the city and coastal plain.
4   Descending slightly, you come to an old concrete bridge over the top of the falls. Although there is no access to the north of the bridge, you can still get good views of the falls from the bridge.
5   A little further on, down some steps, you come to an observation platform. From here, there are extensive views of the city, with its perpendicular tower block thrusting from the surrounding coastal plain. Looking back, you can see the upper falls and the heathland across the valley.
6   Continue the slow descent along the side of the valley. Uphill from the trail, you will see granite outcrops and heath composed of grasstrees, wattles, grevilleas and a multitude of other flowering plants. Downhill there are wandoos on the slopes and marris by the brook. As the trail winds between a cluster of granite rocks, you will see several zamias. Look back to see the entire falls.
7   Cross a small wooden bridge that runs over a floodway. On the opposite side of the valley there is a firebreak or track that winds up the hillside. Continue your descent until it turns right and heads downhill.

8 Take care, as this part of the trail is fairly steep and may be uneven underfoot. The trail winds to the side of the brook, meeting another track that runs along the water's edge. Turn left and follow the track.

9 This section has typical riverside vegetation of marris, sedges and grasses. Opposite, wandoos grow on the rising slope. There are also coral vines (*Kennedia coccinea*) and the rare Helena velvet bush (*Lasiopetalum bracteatum*). Western king parrots can sometimes be seen in the branches of the marris.

10 Kalamunda Shire carpark. Return along the same route to the falls picnic area or arrange for someone to collect you.

David Briggs, Keith Tresidder and Stev Slavin

Where is it? *22 km east of Perth on Falls Road, Lesmurdie.*
Travelling time: *30 minutes from Perth.*
Facilities: *BBQs, tables, water, toilets, carpark.*
On-site information: *Information shelter in picnic area, arrows along trail.*
Best season: *Winter for falls, spring for falls and wildflowers.*

AUSTRALIAN KESTREL

The Australian kestrel (*Falco cenchroides*) is usually seen alone, as it sits quietly on power poles or the very tips of tall trees surveying the surroundings for insects, lizards and small rodents.

These handsome, but small, birds of prey are about 32 centimetres long. The tail, back and wings are a bright rufous brown, marked with black. The underparts are creamy white to the knees, and the rest of the legs are yellow.

Kestrels are often seen in the open grass country along the coast. Many pairs nest in niches in limestone cliffs, either on the mainland or on offshore islands. Inland, the birds lay their eggs in tree hollows, on buildings or on cliff faces.

They are often observed head to wind, hovering with head downturned, looking for prey. When it spies its prey, the bird drops like a stone to impale its chosen morsel on razor sharp talons, then alights to a favoured pole or fence post to dismember the food with its strong curved beak.

34

South Ledge to Golden View Lookout

Length: *600 m return.*
Class: *3.*
Walk time: *30 minutes.*

This walk starts and finishes from the South Ledge picnic site off Mundaring Weir Road. It features magnificent views of the new national park near Mundaring (declared but not formally named at the time of this book going to press) in which this walk is located, and of Mundaring Weir and the historic Golden Pipeline's Number One Pumping Station.

1   Start from the sign saying 'Golden View 300 m', and follow the trail, heading roughly west. After about 50 metres, you will come across a track to your left. This track is the Bibbulmun Track, the long-distance walking track that runs from Kalamunda to Albany. Keep heading straight on, following the directions on the Golden View sign in front of you.
2   This trail follows the contour of the land as it heads around the hill. Looking west, you will get magnificent views down the Helena Valley and over the new national park.
3   After about 150 metres, you come across a small seat and totem pole. This is a great spot to enjoy the views. The granite outcropping you can see through the valley is an important feature of this area. This area is ecologically important, as it lies within the transition from the laterite ridges into granite outcrops which support different plant species.
4   When you're ready to move on again, continue along the track and you will come across some wandoo trees. This is almost the most westerly occurrence of wandoo (*Eucalyptus wandoo*) in the Perth hills area.
5   Soon after passing through the wandoos, you will get your first glimpse of the Mundaring Weir and, shortly afterwards, you arrive at the Golden View Lookout.
6   The Golden View Lookout was a joint project between the Shire of Kalamunda, the Department of Conservation and Land Management (CALM), the Golden Pipeline Project and the Commonwealth Department of Transport and Regional Services. The totem poles that greet you on arrival were completed by arts students at the Kalamunda Senior High School, and feature carvings of many of the animals and plants found in the area. See how many plants and animals you can spot.

7 The view from the Golden View Lookout takes in the Mundaring Weir and Lake C Y O'Connor, adjacent pine plantations, State forest areas and parts of the new national park. The large chimney that is visible is located at the Golden Pipeline's Number One Pumping Station Museum.

8 To return to the South Ledge picnic area, head back the way you came or, alternatively, you can continue down the Bibbulmun Track from the Lookout area to Mundaring Weir (a distance of approximately 1.5 kilometres).

Michael Phillips

Where is it? *40 km east of Perth along Mundaring Weir Road. Turn off to South Ledge/Golden View and a two-way forest road leads about 1 km to South Ledge.*
Travelling time: *1 hour from Perth.*
Facilities: *BBQs, toilet, picnic tables.*
On-site information: *Interpretive information at the lookout.*
Best season: *Spring, early summer.*

CHUDITCH

The chuditch (*Dasyurus geoffroii*) is one of four species of so-called native cats or quolls found in Australia. It is the largest marsupial predator in WA. The chuditch has brown fur with white spots and moves very quickly on the ground, climbs efficiently and may dig or occupy existing holes in the ground. Activity is at its greatest around dawn and dusk.

The term 'cat' is a misnomer, as the chuditch is a marsupial and therefore more closely related to kangaroos and possums. The local Aboriginal name 'chuditch', which mimics the guttural call the animal makes when it is disturbed, is more commonly used.

This aggressive carnivore feeds on a wide variety of small mammals, birds, insects and carrion. Since the arrival of Europeans to this land, poultry runs and rubbish bins have been raided with relish.

The young are carried in a pouch for approximately 11 weeks. By about mid-September they are deposited in a safe den (hollow log or burrow) and can continue to be fed by their mother until they leave the den and disperse around December to January.

Although breeding programs have seen the release of animals back into the wild at several parks and reserves, and trapping has indicated that there are populations in many parts of the south-western corner of WA, the chuditch is still one of our most threatened species.

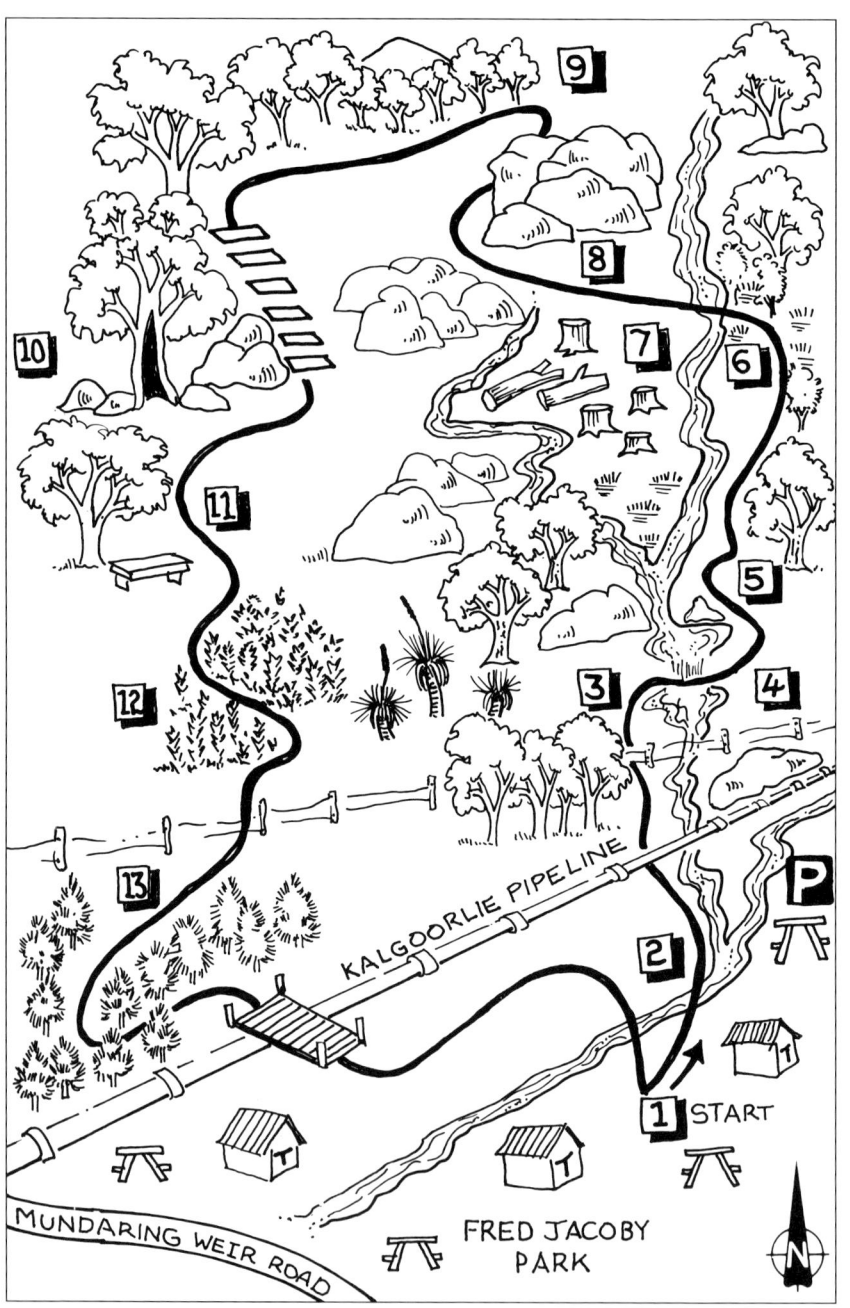

Portagabra Track   **7**

Fred Jacoby Park

Length: *3.8 km loop.*
Class: *4.*
Walk time: *2 hours.*

This challenging walk features granite outcrops, wandoo woodlands and views of Mt Dale to the south-east. It is within a new national park, declared but not formally named at the time of this book going to press.

1 The trail begins at the north-eastern end of Fred Jacoby Park. The area was settled in the 1830s by James Drummond, the Swan River Colony's first botanist. In 1889, the 1124 hectare property was sold to the Jacobys, who named it Portagabra. In 1954, the property was given to the people of WA as a recreation area.

2 The track passes beneath the 557 kilometre long pipeline that supplies water to the Goldfields. Work on the pipeline began in 1898 and was completed in 1903.

3 At this point you can see the remains of an old fenceline on the Portagabra property.

4 After crossing a creek, which flows in winter and early spring, the track narrows and slowly winds along the creek edge.

5 As you meander up a steady rise, the creek is lined with granite outcrops and open wandoo woodland.

6 The track turns to cross the creek at a small soak (wet area) lined with tea trees.

7 From here, the track becomes steeper and moves through jarrah and marri woodland with an understorey of grasstrees. Numerous large stumps scattered through the area are evidence of logging activities around the turn of the century.

8 As the track climbs to the upper slopes of the ridge through a spectacular granite outcrop, the forest to the south-east comes into view. This part of the track is quite steep with several steps. The top of the slope is a good resting spot.

9 The narrow track comes out onto an old track running across the ridge. From here, you can see Mt Dale to the south-east. A short distance along, the track begins to descend steeply and gives spectacular panoramic views.

10 Near the bottom of the slope a large hollow tree stands by the side of the track. It offers shelter to three or four people during rain.

11 A log bench, set beneath the spreading crown of a snottygobble (*Persoonia elliptica*), makes an ideal resting place with views along the creek line.

12 This dense grove of parrotbush (*Dryandra sessilis*) is a favourite habitat for a variety of birds, including splendid wrens, honeyeaters, scarlet robins and larger birds like magpies and twenty-eight parrots.
13 The track continues downwards through the Devenish Plantation, a plantation of *Pinus radiata* established in 1958 and named after Fred Jacoby's daughter Mrs Elfreda Devenish. From here you cross over the pipeline to return to the park.

Jamie Ridley

Where is it? *Fred Jacoby Park, 37 km from Perth on Mundaring Weir Road.*
Travelling time: *45 minutes from Perth.*
Facilities: *BBQs, toilets (suitable for the disabled), carpark.*
On-site information: *Trailhead sign, directional signs along route.*
Best season: *Late winter and spring for wildflowers and running water.*

MOSSES, LIVERWORTS, LICHENS AND FUNGI

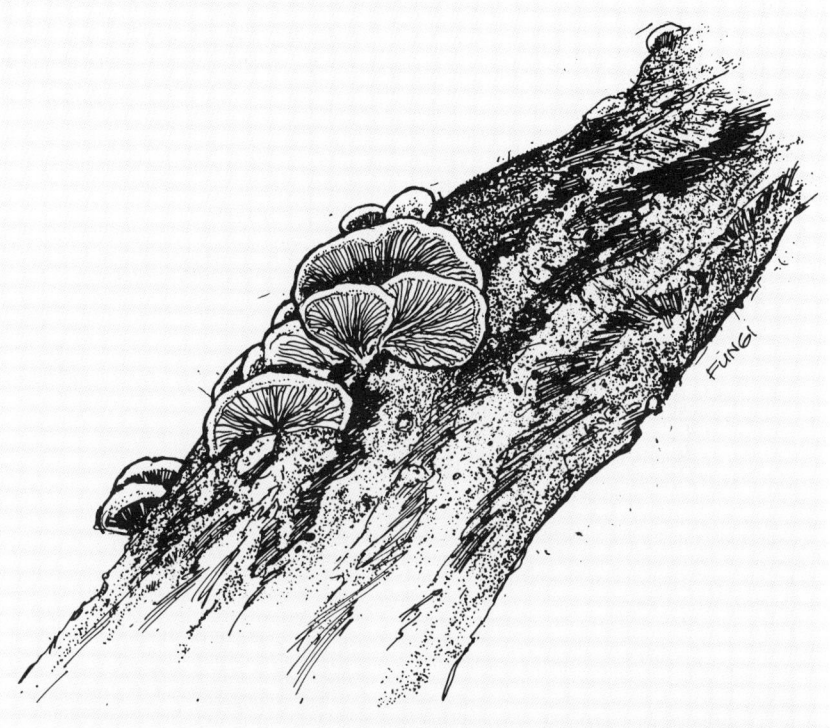

FUNGI

In the plant world, ferns and flowering plants (the vascular plants) usually get the most attention. Because of their size and unusual habitat, the non-vascular plants often go unnoticed. These plants consist of the mosses and liverworts (Bryophites) and the algae, fungi and lichens (Thallophytes).

Mosses, liverworts and lichens frequently form diverse communities on granite rocks throughout the South West of WA.

The mosses and liverworts have a simple form, small size and are quite unrelated to all other general plant life. Lichens are of particular interest because they are composed of alga (green or blue-green) and a fungus.

Mushrooms, toadstools and puffballs (macro-fungi) are usually found on decaying wood, in damp soil and among the leaf litter on the forest floor. In winter, they display a spectacular array of fruiting bodies of all shapes, sizes and colours.

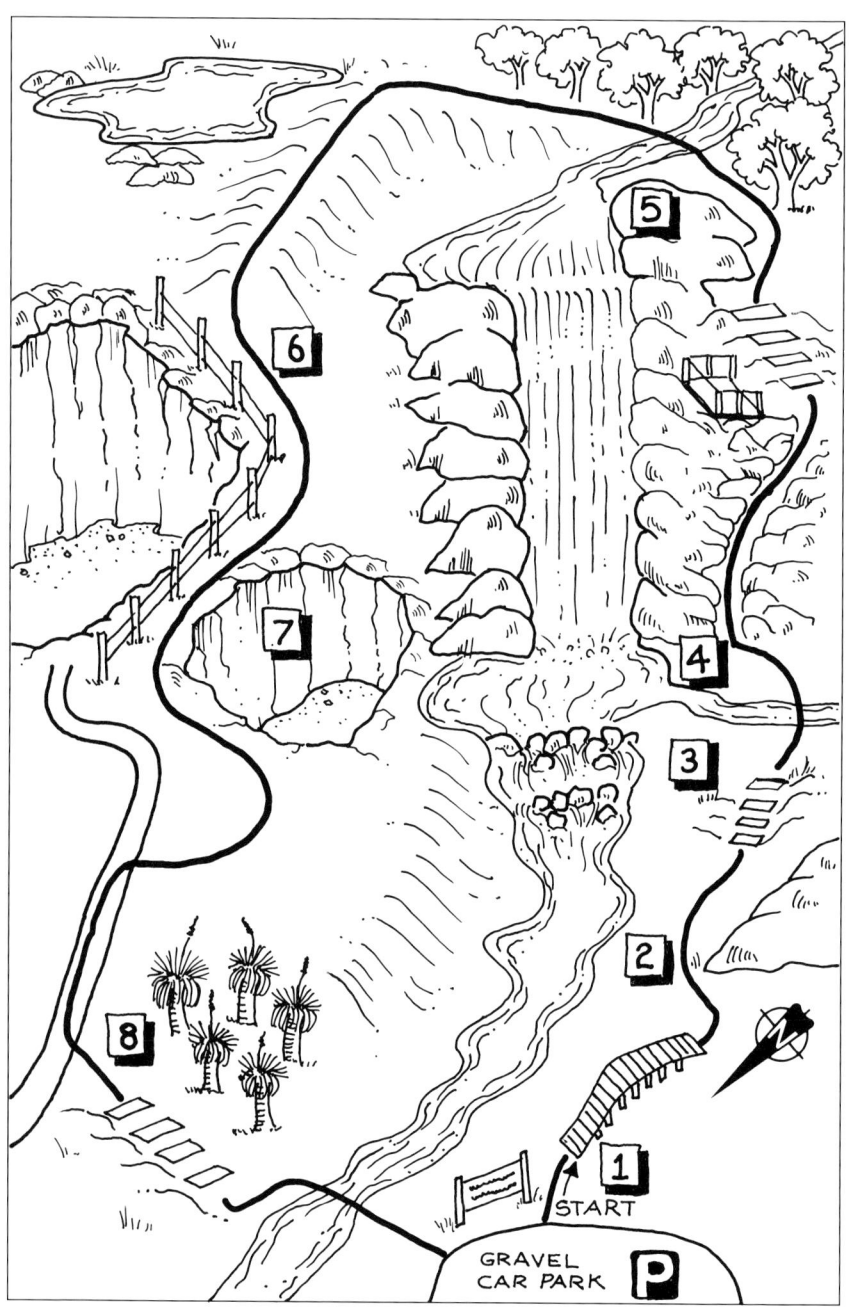

START

GRAVEL
CAR PARK

P

Sixty-foot Falls Walk

8

Ellis Brook Valley Reserve

Length: *2 km loop.*
Class: *3-4.*
Walk time: *1 hour.*

This is the shorter of two walktrails and takes in the falls. It has some steep sections where the ground may be unstable underfoot and walkers should take special care. The falls and wildflowers in spring are the main features of the walk, along with the exposed granite rock of the area, particularly where the brook tumbles over the falls. The area is rich in plant life, and more than 100 different species may easily be observed along the walk.

1   Start from the south-eastern corner of the carpark and proceed straight ahead, over the short bridge towards granite outcrops.
2   Dense closed scrub and colourful heath grows along the stream banks, where the granite outcrops occur. The vegetation on the north and south-facing slopes of the valley is noticeably different because of the differing amounts of sunlight each receives.
3   Close to the small steps, the brook cascades over small rocky shelves.
4   Here, there are excellent views of the falls.
5   From the top of the waterfall there are superb views down the valley to Perth. A very large granite outcrop marks an ideal picnic spot. There is a stand of rare salmon white gum in an area above the falls.
6   There are views into the deep quarry, which was once a source of road-making material. It is now a favourite spot of rock climbers and abseilers.
7   There is a smaller quarry on the left of the track.
8   The track follows the quarry access road for a short distance, before heading down a flight of steps to cross the brook and finish back at the carpark.

Angela Stuart-Street

Where is it? *25 km south of Perth. Access is from Rushton Road.*
Travelling time: *45 minutes from Perth.*
Facilities: *Carpark, picnic spot above the falls.*
On-site information: *Trail markers in places along route.*
Best season: *All year, spring for wildflowers.*

43

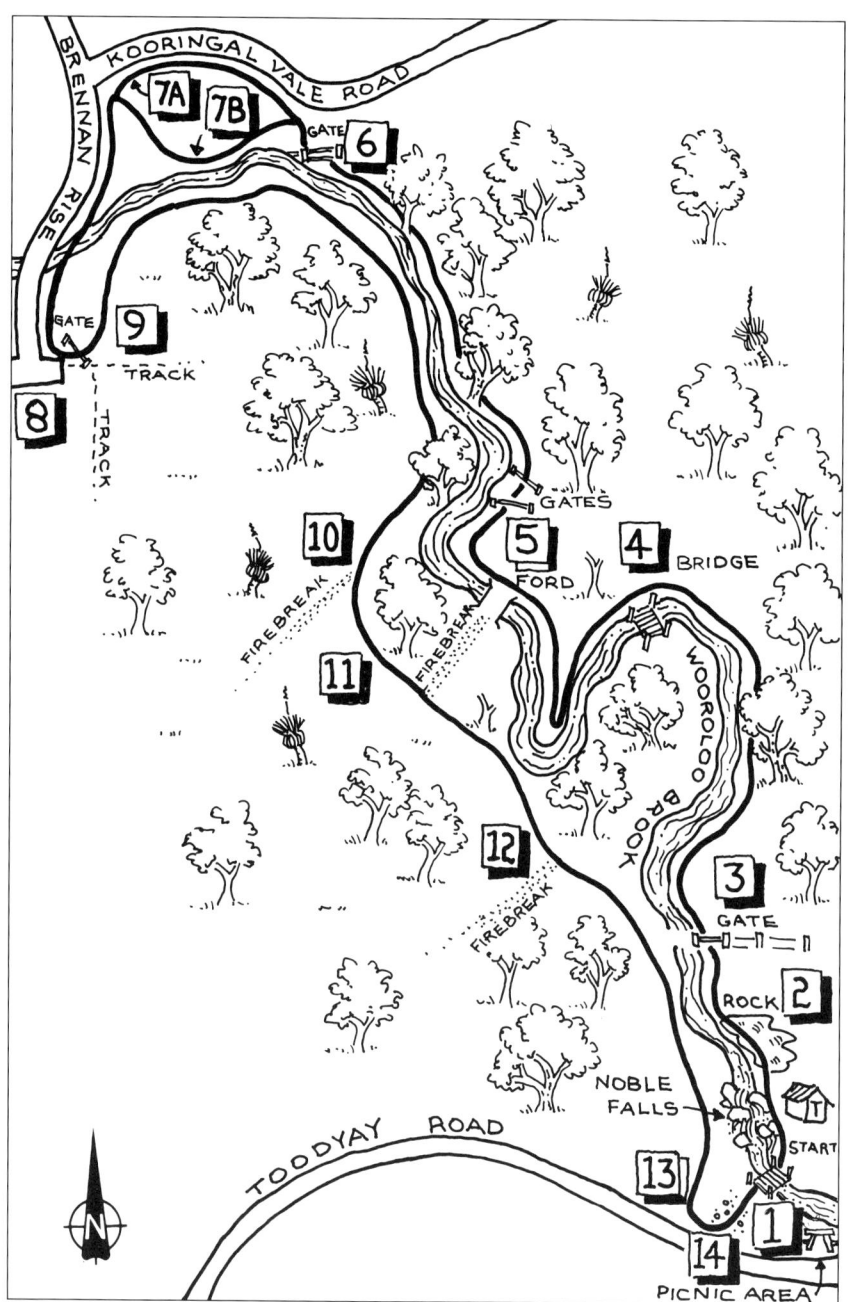

Noble Falls Walk

Length: *3.5 km.*
Class: *3. Flat walk most of the way. Good surface.*
Walk time: *45 minutes.*

This walk along the Wooroloo Brook is attractive year round. Wildflowers bloom in spring, and a stunning waterfall flows at Noble Falls in winter and spring. The walk adjoins a reserve, which is home to abundant wildlife. It begins from the Noble Falls picnic and parking area (directly opposite the Noble Falls Hotel) off Toodyay Road.

1   The falls are visible from the carpark. Cross the footbridge and then turn left, following the Wooroloo Brook and heading past Noble Falls.
2   The path will come to a large sheet of rock. Cross over the rock.
3   Continue along the path until you pass through a gate.
4   On the left, you will notice a footbridge going over the creek. (Note: crossing this bridge and turning left is a short walk of 1.3 kilometres).
5   With the ford on your left, turn right through a gate, then left through another.
6   Go through the gate up to the bitumen road (Kooringal Vale Drive) then turn left.
7A Wet weather route: follow the road to the T-junction (Brennan Rise).
7B Dry weather route: walk several metres and then walk left down the road embankment to 'Kangaroo' Track, which then becomes a firebreak. At the end of the firebreak, walk up the embankment to the road (Kooringal Vale Drive). Follow the road to the T-junction (Brennan Rise).
8   When you reach the T-junction at Old Coach Road, turn left through the gate.
9   Turn left again, into the lower firebreak.
10 The path joins the higher firebreak. Turn left.
11 Turn left back to the lower firebreak.
12 Take the left fork.
13 Walk up the road embankment to Toodyay Road, watching for traffic. Turn left.
14 Turn left down the embankment and return to the picnic area. Take care as the gravel is very slippery.

Simona Willis

Where is it? *About 50 km north-east of Perth, near Gidgegannup.*
Travelling time: *1 hour, 20 minutes from Perth via Toodyay Road.*
Facilities: *Picnic tables, toilets, BBQs.*
On-site information: *Markers along trail.*

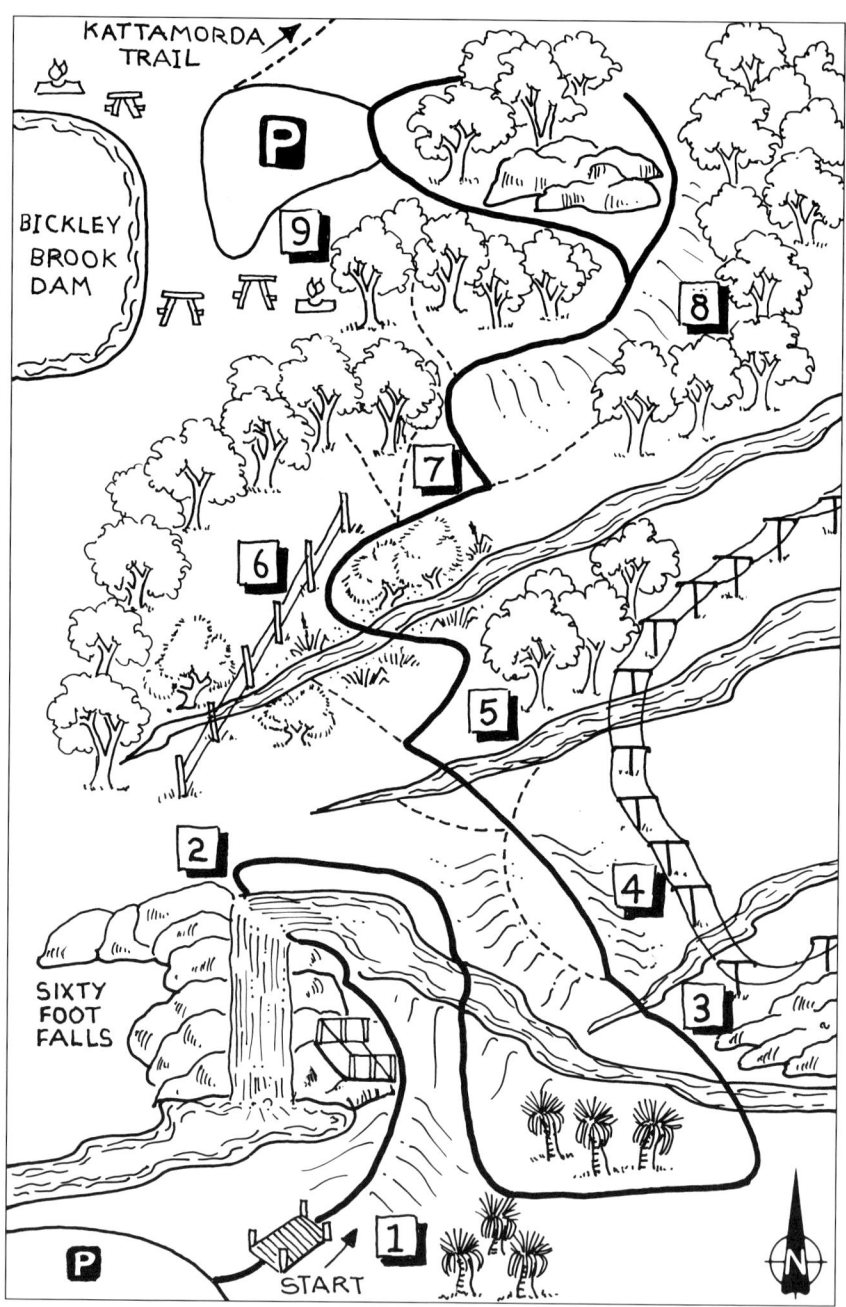

KATTAMORDA TRAIL

P

9

BICKLEY BROOK DAM

8

7

6

5

4

3

2

SIXTY FOOT FALLS

1

START

P

N

Valley to Valley Walk 10

Ellis Brook

Length: *8 km one-way.*
Class: *4.*
Walk time: *3-4 hours.*

This is a pleasant one-way walk from Ellis Brook to Bickley Dam. You will need to arrange transport at the other end. The walk features wildflowers (in spring), jarrah forest, views over both valleys and rocky outcrops. The last two or three kilometres is particularly attractive as you descend to Bickley Dam. The City of Gosnells organises an annual conducted walk along this route during the wildflower season (phone Community Programs at the Council offices for further details).

Note: Bickley Dam is a water catchment area, in which dogs are not allowed.

1   Starting from the carpark, cross the footbridge and follow the track along the creek to just past the first fork, where there are good views across to the falls. From here, there is a well-rewarded steep climb up to the falls.
2   There are delightful views looking over the valley towards the city from above the falls. Cross the creek, take a right turn and follow the track east along the edge of the creek. The track then crosses the creek and continues east until it meets a powerline, swings north to cross the creek once more and follows the powerline.
3   The large granite outcrop on your right makes a good spot for a rest and some refreshment. Take care not to damage the fragile vegetation growing on the rock.
4   After a short while, the track leaves the powerline and turns left to a ridgetop. This stretch features distant views over tree tops.
5   Just beyond the small creek, there are excellent views west over the city. Continue along the ridge and walk towards a wide creek ahead and a fenceline on your left.
6   The track crosses the creek. Its sandy banks are lined with old paperbarks and reeds.
7   At this point you get your first glimpse into the valleys that weave away to the east, with a flush of green tree cover. Just beyond is a three-way intersection and you should take the track to the north-east. Turn left at the next main intersection and right at the one after that.

8   Standing on the ridgetop, surrounded by attractive dense jarrah forest, you have excellent views over Bickley Valley. Continue along the track with the rock outcrop to your right. After passing the rock you have a clear view down the valley.

9   Bickley Dam. Lunch beside the dam is a pleasant end to an enjoyable walk.

Fiona Marr, Tracy Churchill, Janet Walker

Where is it? *25 km south of Perth. Access is from Rushton Road.*
Travelling time: *45 minutes from Perth.*
Facilities: *Carparks at both ends (check closing time), BBQs and tables at Bickley Dam.*
On-site information: *Silver trail markers in places along route.*
Best season: *Autumn, spring for wildflowers.*

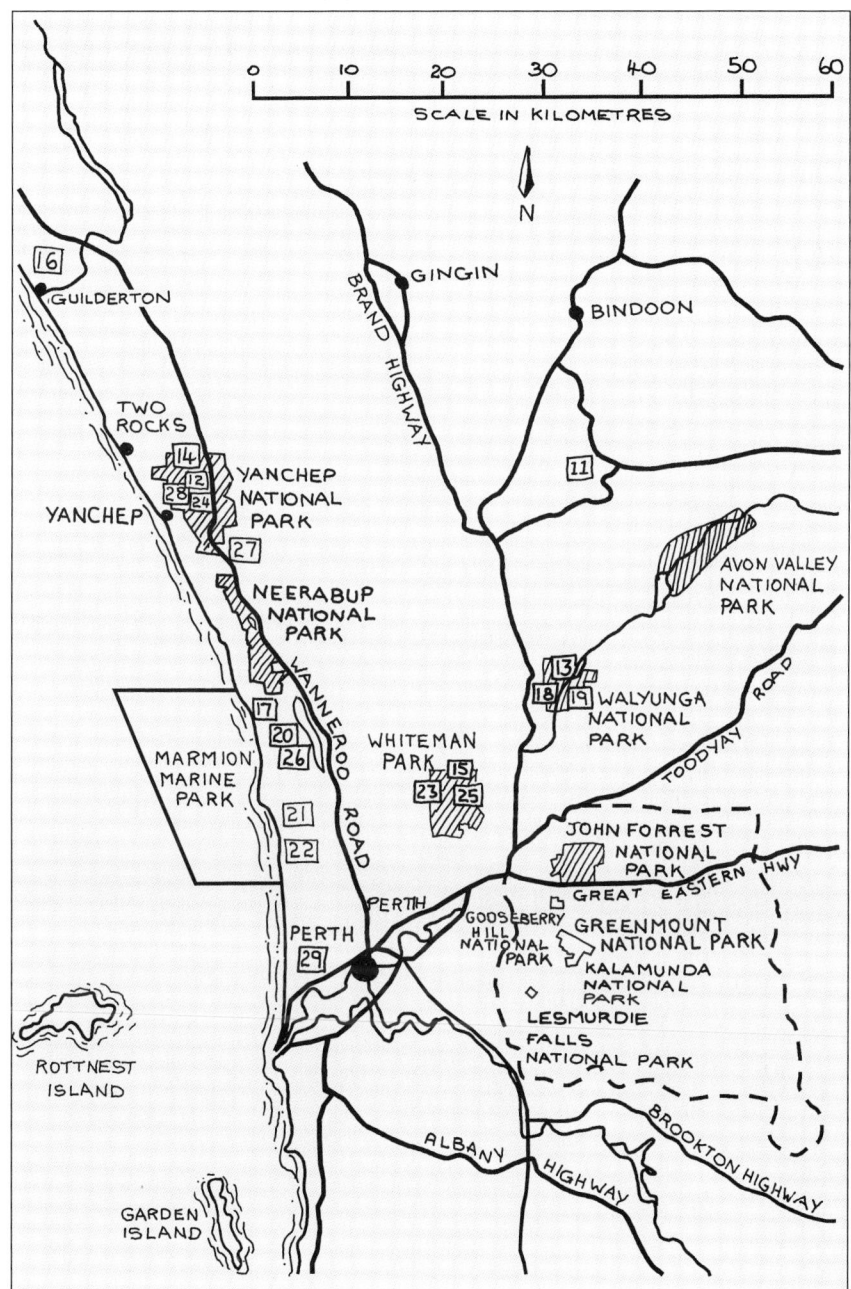

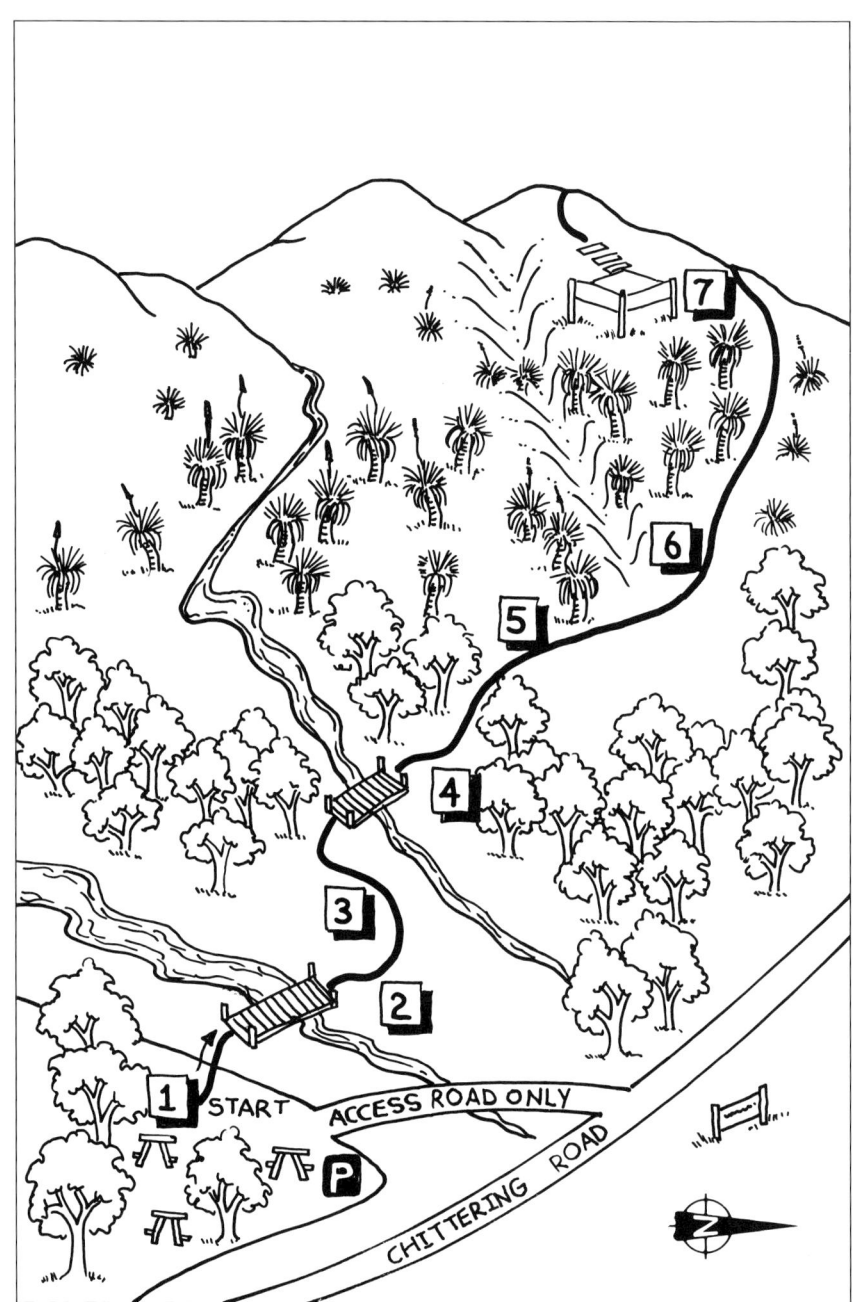

START

ACCESS ROAD ONLY

CHITTERING ROAD

Blackboy Ridge Walktrail

Length: *1.5 km return.*
Class: *3.*
Walk time: *45 minutes (with stop at lookout).*

This pleasant walk is good at any time of the year, but it is truly spectacular during early spring when wildflowers are abundant. The hillside is covered with wattles, parrotbush, delicate orchids and, of course, hundreds of grasstrees, which give the area its name. The trail follows a well-worn route that rises steadily up the hill to a lookout.

1   Start from the northern end of the small picnic area, where there is a wooden 'walktrail' sign.
2   Very soon you will cross a footbridge over a small creek.
3   The lower slopes of the ridge support a woodland of marri and wandoo, with its attendant understorey of heath plants.
4   A second footbridge crosses a very small creek, which is dry for most of the year.
5   The marri-wandoo woodland thins out and heath vegetation becomes more dominant as you climb the gentle slope of the trail. The upper slopes are dominated by grasstrees.
6   Looking uphill to the left of the track, there is a depression in the hillside which is covered in grasstrees. It looks particularly attractive in spring.
7   On the final ascent, the trail passes briefly around the side of the ridge before crossing the summit and leading down to a lookout. From here, there are spectacular views across the Chittering Valley.

David Gough, Victoria Maxwell

Where is it? *70 km north of Perth in the Chittering Valley.*
Travelling time: *1 hour, 20 minutes from Perth.*
Facilities: *Picnic area, carpark.*
On-site information: *Signs from road and carpark.*
Best season: *All year, spring for wildflowers.*

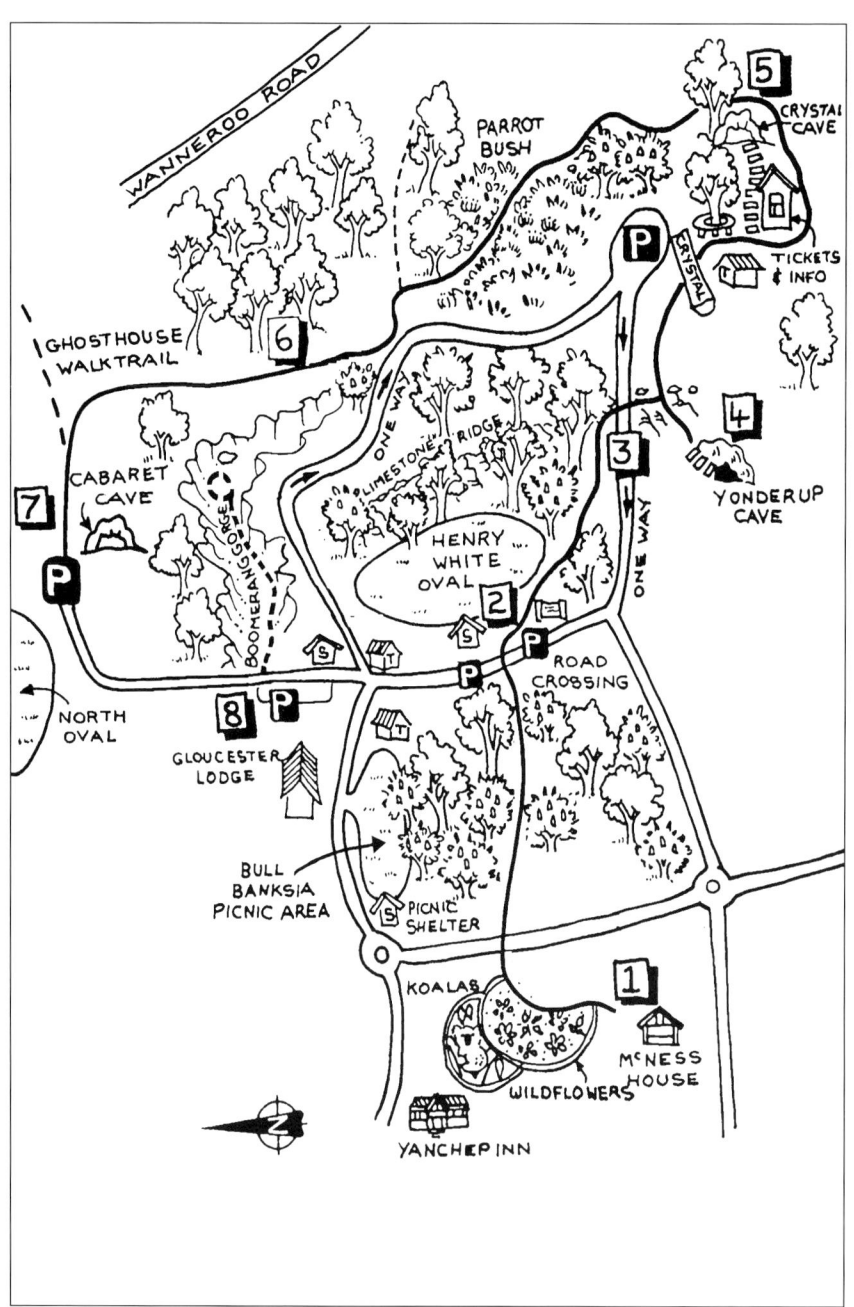

Caves Walktrail

12

Yanchep National Park ($)

Length: *4.5 km circuit.*
Class: *3. Some rocky and uneven surfaces.*
Walk time: *2 hours (or 3 hours with a guided tour of Crystal Cave).*

This trail is an excellent way to find out about the caves in Yanchep National Park and how they were formed. Please take care, as some sections are rocky and many limestone caves and crevices are hidden by the undergrowth.

1   Begin at McNess Visitor Centre. Follow the 'cave' markers through to Henry White Oval. Take care when crossing roads.
2   Follow the limestone trail around the back of the goal posts.
3   Enter the tuart woodland. These large trees generally grow in rocky limestone soils, and require a steady flow of underground water. Where tuarts grow on rocky outcrops, they are a good indicator that limestone caves lie below. Follow the trail to the road. Look out for cars when crossing.
4   Follow the path to an intersection. Turn right and walk 70 metres to the entrance of Yonderup Cave. Yonderup has been a popular tourist cave since the 1930s. It closed in 1984 for renovations and to allow for further archaeological studies (Aboriginal bones were discovered in a chamber in 1948). The cave is now open for small organised tours (enquire at McNess Visitor Centre, bookings required). Retrace your steps to the intersection and continue on to Crystal Cave.
5   Crystal Cave has been open to the public since the 1930s. Take a guided tour (45 minutes – bookings can be made at McNess Visitor Centre before heading off), then walk to the back of the ticket office and follow the markers.
6   After several hundred metres, the trail will take you left, descending towards the edge of Boomerang Gorge. This gorge follows an ancient stream bed and is believed to be a collapsed cave system. Follow markers to the right.
7   Cross over an old vehicle track. Further along, the trail joins up with the Ghost House Walktrail. Turn left to finish the trail at North Oval and Cabaret Cave.
8   You may want to take a short detour into Boomerang Gorge along the Dwerta Mia Walktrail (500 metres, 20 minutes return) starting from the Boomerang Gorge carpark. Otherwise, follow the road that runs past the ornamental lakes, Gloucester Lodge and the Yanchep Inn to return to the lake foreshore.

Therese Jones, Christie Mahony

Where is it? *Yanchep National Park, 51 km north of Perth on Wanneroo Road.*
Travelling time: *1 hour from Perth.*
Facilities: *BBQs, picnic shelters, toilets.*
Best season: *All year. Tours of Crystal Cave run every day of the year!*

WA CHRISTMAS TREE

CHRISTMAS TREE

Western Australia is lucky enough to have its own Christmas tree, a mistletoe, which in early summer bursts into a profusion of brilliant orange flowers and heralds the approaching festive season.

The WA Christmas tree (*Nuytsia floribunda*) is botanically an unusual tree. It has no close relatives and is classed in a genus by itself. It is the only mistletoe to grow as a tree. All other mistletoes grow on the branches of trees.

This species usually has a well-developed trunk that becomes very thick in relation to the tree's size. The branches are also thick and bend under the weight of the bluish-green foliage and the flowers, which are held at the end of the branchlets. The trunk of the tree, however, is not true wood, but a starchy tissue that is often gnawed by farm animals, sometimes right through.

WA Christmas trees are semi-parasitic. Their roots make rings around those of nearby plants and suckers within the rings extract water from them.

New plants can sprout from a large network of underground stems. As a result, groups of saplings are often seen around natural specimens.

The WA Christmas tree ranges from Kalbarri to Israelite Bay. It is common in almost all soil types on the coastal plain, particularly in low-lying areas. In the Darling Range, it grows chiefly in rocky or damp places.

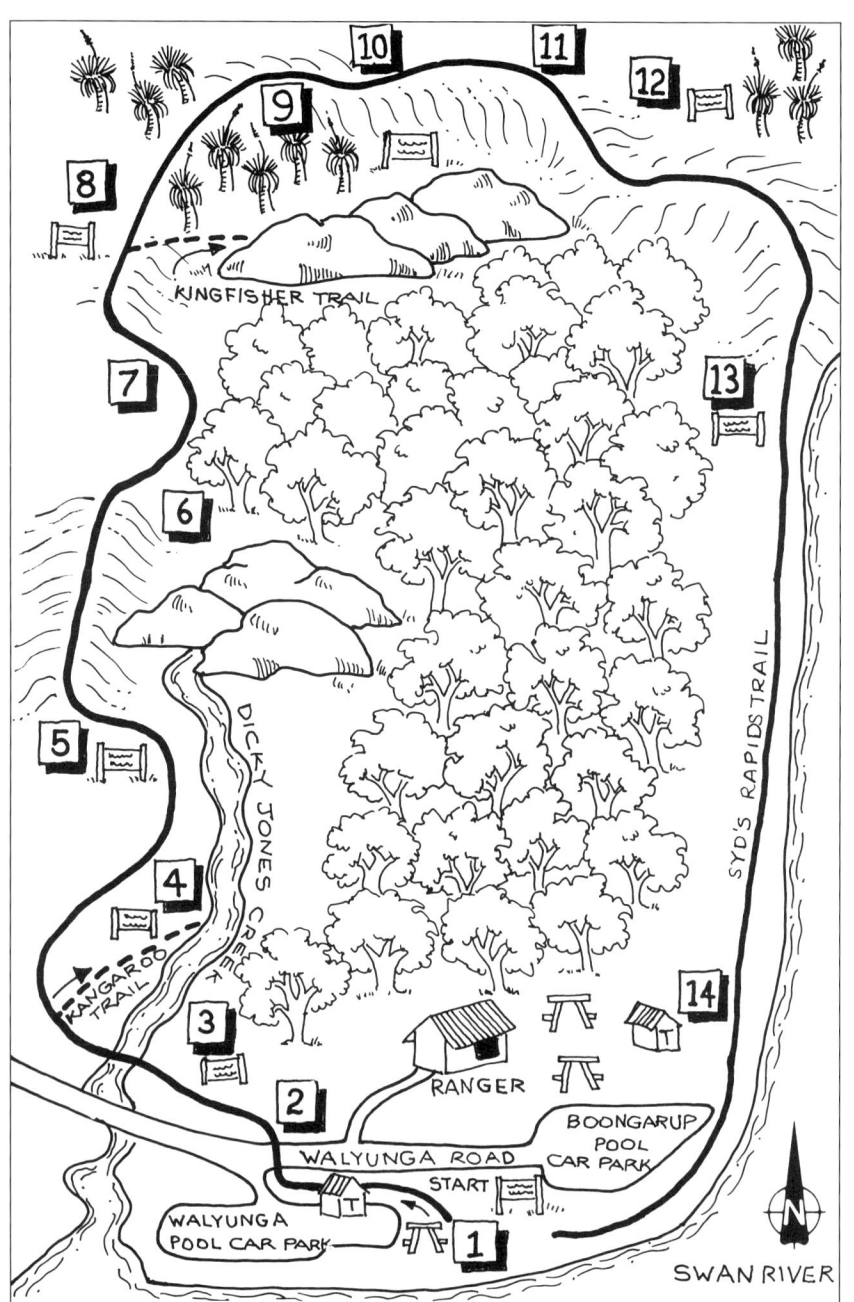

KINGFISHER TRAIL

DICKY JONES CREEK

KANGAROO TRAIL

SYD'S RAPIDS TRAIL

RANGER

WALYUNGA ROAD

START

WALYUNGA POOL CAR PARK

BOONGARUP POOL CAR PARK

SWAN RIVER

N

Echidna Trail

13

Walyunga National Park ($)

Length: *10.6 km loop.*
Class: *4.*
Walk time: *4 hours, 30 minutes.*

This trail, which was made possible with assistance from Rotary International, offers walkers the chance to enjoy a variety of wildflowers at close quarters. There are some interesting granite outcrops and, although most of the trees in the area are wandoo and marri, you will see some small stands of jarrah on the high laterite ridges.

1 The trail begins as the Kangaroo Trail in the carpark at Walyunga Pool.
2 Follow the kangaroo markers and cross over the road into wandoo-marri woodland.
3 Cross Dicky Jones Creek for information about an old dwelling that was in the area.
4 At the start of the Echidna Trail there is an information panel about walktrail options. Follow the pink Echidna Trail markers.
5 An information panel near a wandoo explains how the tree provides habitat for numerous animals and birds.
6 This spot provides scenic views over the valley and photographic opportunities.
7 Another vantage point provides sweeping views over the Swan Coastal Plain.
8 At the junction with the Kingfisher Trail there is another information panel with details of walktrail options.
9 An information panel in Dicky Jones Gully tells the story of the Aboriginal significance of the area. Many large grasstrees can be seen here.
10 Woodsome Hill, the highest point in the park at 260 metres above sea level, is clearly visible. An information panel gives more details.
11 This is another good spot for views across the Avon Valley.
12 As the trail descends to the river, the railway line which runs through the Avon Valley becomes visible. An information board gives more details.
13 At this point, the Echidna Trail joins Syd's Rapids Trail and continues along the river's edge. An information panel gives details of how the rapids got their name.
14 Syd's Rapids Trail joins the Aboriginal Heritage Trail, which runs back to the start at Walyunga Pool picnic area. Interpretive panels along the trail give details of the Aboriginal heritage values of the park.

Ross McGill, Steve Strachan

Where is it? *40 km north-east of Perth via the Great Northern Highway and Walyunga Road.*

Travelling time: *1 hour from Perth.*

Facilities: *BBQs, toilets and water at both picnic areas in the park.*

On-site information: *Trailhead sign, pink echidna markers and interpretive panels.*

Best season: *All year except hot summer days, especially spring for wildflowers and winter for fast-flowing river.*

ECHIDNA

ECHIDNA

One of the world's most primitive mammals is widely distributed through-out Australia and inhabits outer urban areas of Perth. The short-beaked echidna (*Tachyglossus aculeatus*), recognisable by its covering of long spines, has been seen waddling down suburban streets in Woodvale and turns up occasionally in backyards in the suburbs of Kalamunda and Armadale.

The echidna is one of only two Australian monotremes, or egg-laying mammals. The other is the platypus.

Female monotremes lay a soft-shelled egg and suckle their young on milk secreted through numerous ducts opening onto the abdomen. The egg is probably laid directly into the pouch on the belly of the female. It hatches after ten days and the young remains there for a further three months.

A highly specialised feeder, the echidna exposes termite galleries by breaking open nests with its strong forepaws or snout, or by digging into soil, and extracts termites with its long sticky tongue.

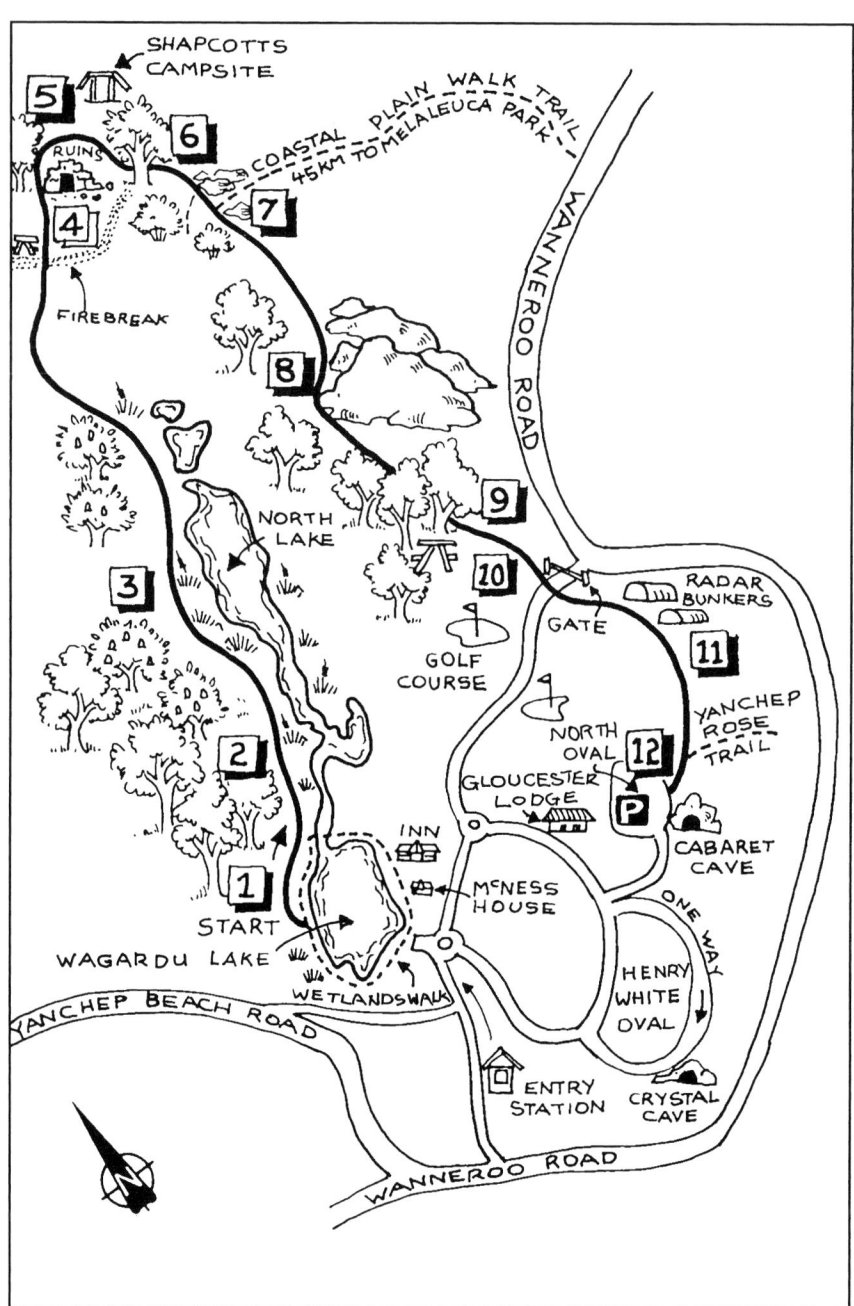

SHAPCOTTS CAMPSITE

5

6

7

COASTAL PLAIN WALK TRAIL
45KM TO MELALEUCA PARK

WANNEROO ROAD

RUINS

4

FIREBREAK

8

NORTH LAKE

3

9

RADAR BUNKERS

10

GATE

11

GOLF COURSE

YANCHEP ROSE TRAIL

2

NORTH OVAL

12

GLOUCESTER LODGE

P

CABARET CAVE

1

START

INN

ONE WAY

WAGARDU LAKE

McNESS HOUSE

HENRY WHITE OVAL

WETLANDS WALK

YANCHEP BEACH ROAD

ENTRY STATION

CRYSTAL CAVE

WANNEROO ROAD

Ghost House Trail 14

Yanchep National Park ($)

Length: *9.2 km.*
Class: *3 (some rocky terrain).*
Walk time: *4 hours, 30 minutes.*

The Ghost House Trail offers some of the best 'wilderness' walking in Yanchep National Park. It takes you on a natural and cultural journey around the park's most pristine wetlands, namely Wagardu Lake (Loch McNess) and North Lake. The trail starts on the western side of Wagardu Lake (one kilometre along the Wetlands Walktrail) and finishes at the North Oval carpark near Cabaret Cave. The trail passes through grand examples of tuart forest, banksia woodlands and coastal heath. The rocky limestone outcrops are a special feature along the trail and provide scenic vistas of the North Lake and its surrounds. Walkers can visit the historic ruins of the Ghost House and the Chauffeur's Quarters (a spur trail). Better still, make your walk an overnighter by camping out at the new and fully equipped Shapcotts campsite, which includes a hikers' hut, water tank, picnic tables and a toilet.

IMPORTANT: Please sign on at the WALKSAFE register box at McNess House Visitor Centre before commencing this walk, and remember to check back in on your return.

1   To begin, follow the Wetlands Walktrail for about one kilometre and then turn left onto the Ghost House Trail. You will begin to ascend, walking up through some of the oldest examples of tuart forest in the park. The tuart (*Eucalyptus gomphocephala*) has rough grey bark. If you look into the canopy you may notice some dead branches, the result of a hot wildfire in 1991.

2   As you wind your way around the lake's edge, the trail gently climbs higher onto a limestone ridge. While you do this you may notice the vegetation changing from tuart forest to lower banksia woodlands and dense parrotbush (*Dryandra sessilis*). This high shrub has prickly, fan-shaped leaves and creamy yellow (sweet smelling) flower heads. The flowers provide an abundance of pollen and nectar for insects and birds. If you walk quietly through this area you may observe ringneck parrots or Carnaby's (white-tailed) black-cockatoos feeding busily in the thickets.

3   As you walk along the edge of the ridge, you will catch glimpses of North Lake on your right. This natural wetland is predominantly covered by dense sedges and small pockets of open water. Before European settlement, Yanchep was inhabited

by the Nyoongar people. They regularly burnt the bulrush along the lake (*Typha orientalis*), an important food source, to improve its growth. Today this lake is a conservation sanctuary for wetland birds. Listen carefully as you make your way down to the water's edge. You may hear the unusual shrill call of the musk duck, which has a distinct skin-like bag hanging from its throat.

4   Continue along the lake's edge until you reach two large flame trees and a picnic table next to a major firebreak. Cross the firebreak. Directly ahead is a limestone wall with a doorframe, shaded by large flame trees. This is the 'Ghost House', the remains of Mr L Shapcott's weekender (a similar style to McNess House) built during the park's development as a health and pleasure resort during the 1930s. Only ruins lie here today.

5   As you walk past the ruins, you will notice a trailhead sign for the Coastal Plain Walktrail. This long-distance trail stretches from Yanchep National Park to Melaleuca Park, a distance of 46 kilometres. The Ghost House Trail joins the start of this trail, so that all walkers can use the campsite facilities. The campsite is named Shapcotts to commemorate Mr Shapcott's work in the park.

6   Return to the trail behind the camp shelter and follow the yellow markers onto the vehicle track into a head high thicket of wattle.

7   You begin to scamper up a rocky section of track. At this point, the two trails split. The Ghost House Trail follows a vehicle track to the right and the Coastal Plain Walktrail splits to the left.

8   As you walk along, there are some rocky limestone outcrops to your left. Along these ridges and below your feet is a vast network of caves. The caves have been created by a complex system of natural streams. The water that moves through the park is from a large aquifer called the Gnangara Mound. The chain of wetlands along the coastal plain are all recharged by this enormous aquifer.

9   The trail winds through denser forest with plenty of bird life. Take a rest in the sunken hollow to the right. In spring, native wisteria (*Hardenbergia comptoniana*) and white clematis (*Clematis pubescens*) mix with the wattle.

10 Further along, you'll see the golf course on your right. Cross the road and continue along a track.

11 Follow the track past the concrete generator huts which were used to power the radar huts during World War II.

12 Nice views can be gained from the ridge before the trail rejoins the Yanchep Rose Trail (red markers). Follow the yellow markers back to the North Oval and Cabaret Cave. To return to the foreshore, take the road that runs past the ornamental lakes, Gloucester Lodge and the Yanchep Inn.

Therese Jones, Christie Mahoney

Where is it? *Yanchep National Park, 51 km north of Perth on Wanneroo Road.*
Travelling time: *1 hour, 10 minutes.*
Facilities: *Picnic area, toilets, carpark in the park.*
On-site information: *Yellow markers along trail.*
Best season: *All year except hot summer days.*

BUSH BOOKS

How can you tell a humpback from a southern right whale, a jarrah from a marri or a kestrel from a kite? It's easy when you are travelling with a set of **Bush Books**!

Bush Books are a series of practical field guides to help people discover the State's unique plants, animals and special features, region by region. More than 30 titles have been released, and more are planned.

Bush Books are pocket-sized, and each is based around a defined geographic region, which contributes to their ease of use. The books are inexpensive and readily available from many outlets, including most bookshops, CALM offices, RAC shops, many tourist information centres and other specialist outlets, such as camping shops. All but one are in full colour.

Titles relevant to the Perth area include:

Bugs in the Backyard
Birds in the Backyard
Bush Tucker Plants of the South-West
Beachcomber's Guide to South-West Beaches
Common Trees of the South-West Forests
Common Wildflowers of the South-West Forests
Common Birds of the South-West Forests
Mammals of the South-West
Whales and Dolphins of Western Australia
Rare Birds of Western Australia
Western Australian Birds of Prey

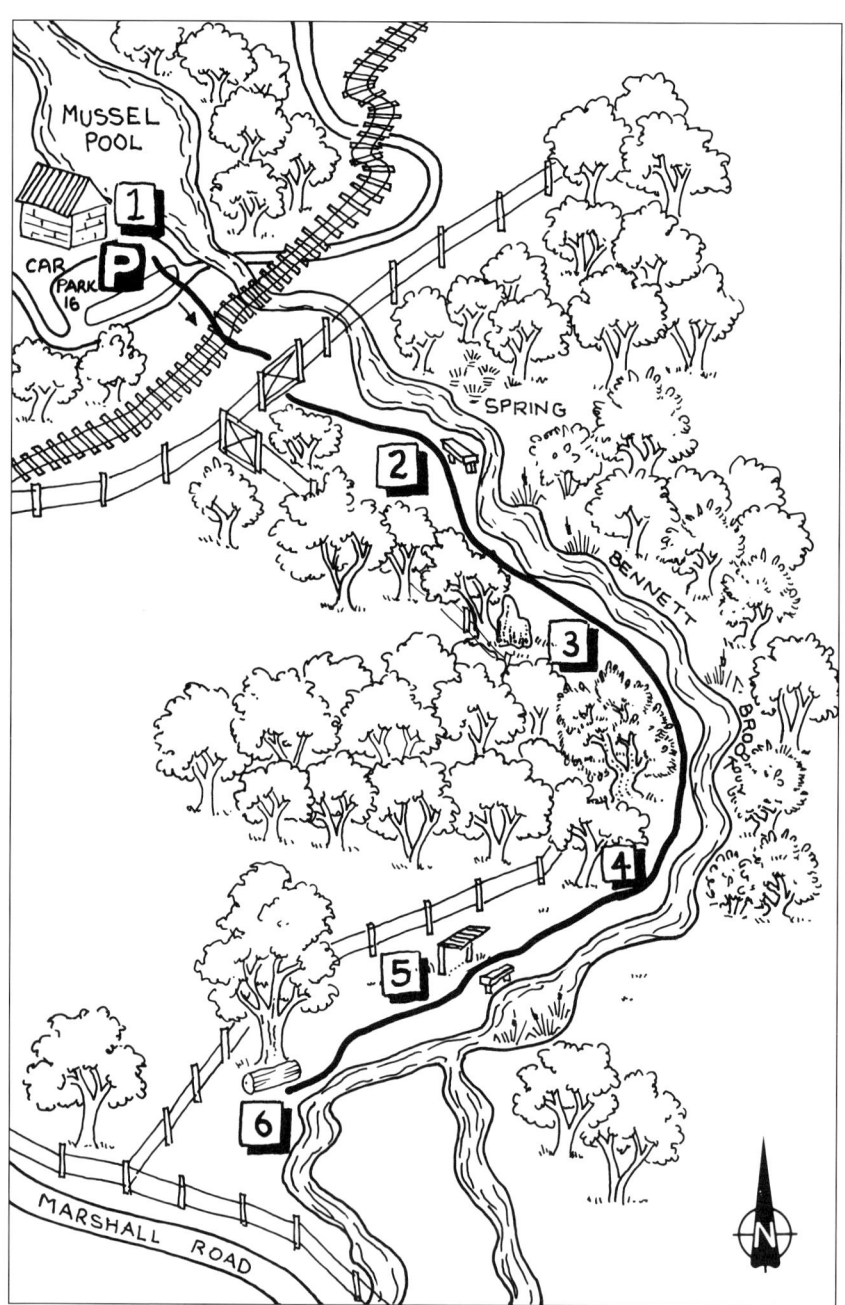

Goo-loorto Walktrail

15

Whiteman Park ($)

Length: *3 km return.*
Class: *3.*
Walk time: *1 hour, 15 minutes.*

'Goo-loorto' means 'a species of eucalypt' in the Nyoongar language of the area. This probably refers to the flooded gum (*Eucalyptus rudis*), and many large and splendid examples of this tree can be seen beside this trail. The trail is along the western side of Bennett Brook, the outflow of Mussel Pool and Horse Swamp. The northern portion of the brook usually dries up to isolated pools by early December, and starts to flow again with rains in May/June. The southern portion near Marshall Road usually flows all year, as it is fed by seepage from the Gnangara Mound.

1   Begin at the log cabin by Mussel Pool.
2   After about 300 metres, the trail passes a permanent spring (trail marker 'G'). It is on the eastern side of the brook and only readily accessible during summer.
3   At 'H' there is a large termite mound around the base of a flooded gum. A little further on, the trail passes an unusually large freshwater paperbark ('I').
4   Several very large stout paperbarks (*Melaleuca preissiana*) can also be seen along the trail, whilst in August and September a grove of coojong or golden wreath wattles (*Acacia saligna*) make a splendid sight in full flower.
5   The last 300 metres is through open grassland, as most of the trees and shrubs were cleared in the 1940s for grazing. The brook was excavated here, also in the 1940s, to create a dam ('J') for watering cattle. It became choked with the introduced bulrush (*Typha orientalis*), but this has almost been eradicated and replaced with native reeds. An ongoing program of revegetation on each side of the brook will see a range of wildlife habitats restored. Ground near the brook is low-lying and swampy, with some patches of introduced edible watercress.
6   The trail ends 200 metres north of the Marshall Road fenceline, beneath a large marri. A log has been placed here so walkers can rest awhile. There is no access to Marshall Road: you must return to Mussel Pool along the same route.

Dave Bright

Where is it? *18 km north of Perth. Entrance off Lord Street, West Swan.*
Travelling time: *25 minutes from Perth.*
Facilities: *BBQs, tables, toilets, carparks, picnic shelters.*
On-site information: *Trailhead sign, red painted posts along trail.*

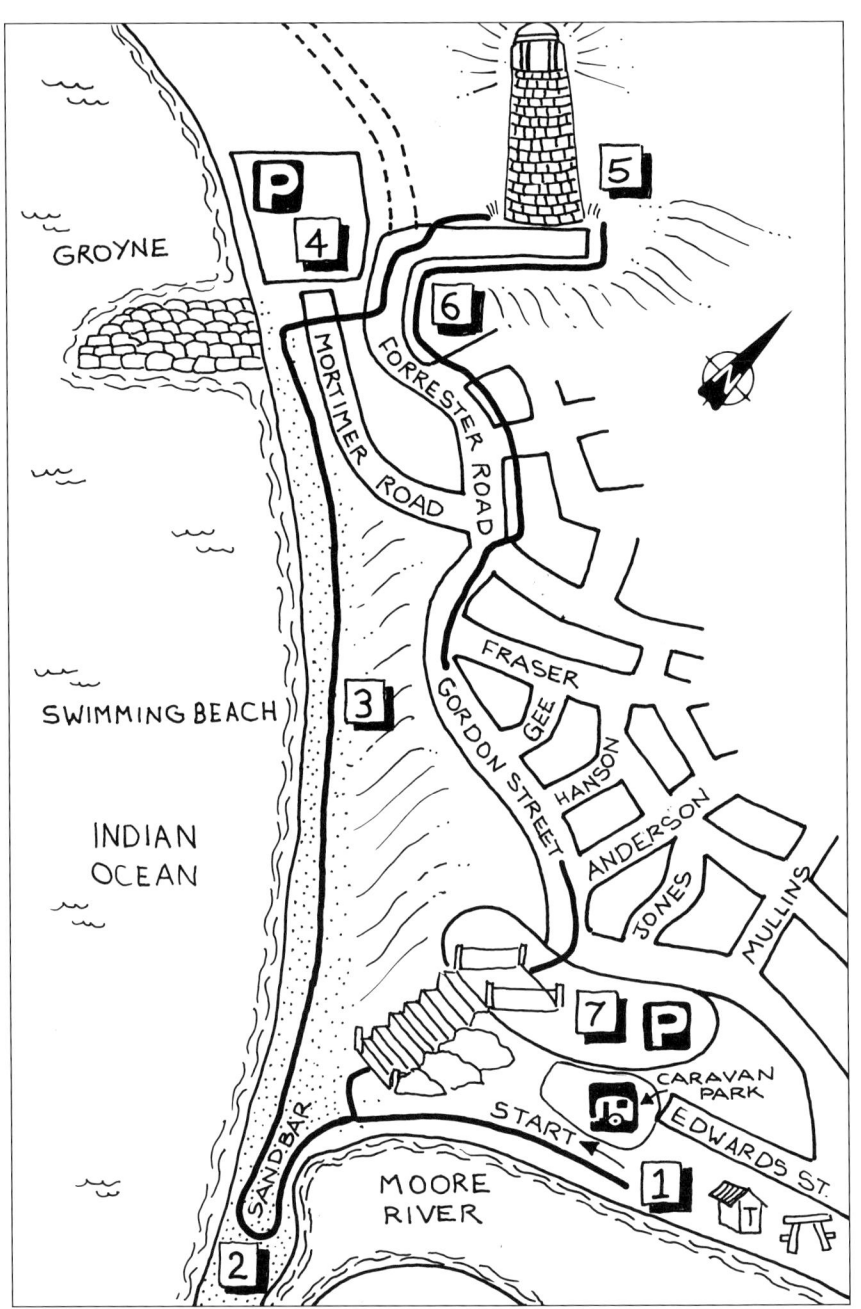

GROYNE

SWIMMING BEACH

INDIAN
OCEAN

MORTIMER ROAD

FORRESTER ROAD

GORDON STREET

FRASER

GEE

HANSON

ANDERSON

JONES

MULLINS

CARAVAN PARK

EDWARDS ST.

START

SAND BAR

MOORE RIVER

P
P

4
5
6
3
7
1
2

Guilderton Lighthouse Trail

16

Length: *4.3 km loop.*
Class: *3.*
Walk time: *2 hours.*

The trail runs from the main picnic area, along the river and beach up to the impressive red brick lighthouse that stands high above the limestone cliff.

1   From the picnic area, proceed along the river's edge to the sandbar at the mouth of the Moore River. There are pleasant views across the river to the ocean.
2   The Moore River is sealed by a sandbar at various times of the year, depending on seasonal rains. The sandbar usually closes the river mouth during the summer months and is generally passable except during high tides. Crossing should not be attempted at any time when the river is open to the sea.
3   Proceed along the beach heading north towards the old groyne, which is clearly visible. This is a delightful stretch of beach that offers scenic grandeur and good swimming (when appropriate).
4   The groyne provides parking for vehicles and has scenic views. From here, climb uphill to Forrester Road and head towards the lighthouse.
5   The lighthouse is built in red brick to a height of 31 metres. There is no access into the lighthouse compound itself, but there are excellent views from Tank Road. Wildflowers abound during spring and you may see some bobtail skinks along the track.
6   Return along Forrester Road and Mortimer Road before turning into Gordon Street. This is also a good area for wildflowers in spring.
7   The lookout, near Gordon Street carpark, provides panoramic views over the ocean, the river and the Guilderton townsite. While there, take the time to inspect the shipwreck plinth. Walk down the steps to the beach and return to the picnic area via the riverside beach.

Richard Hammond, Meryl Nolan, Joanne Chadwick

Where is it? *97 km north of Perth. Picnic area in Edwards Street.*
Travelling time: *1 hour from Perth via Wanneroo Road.*
Facilities: *BBQs, playground, shelters, shop, toilets and a caravan park, including on-site accommodation.*
Best season: *All year, spring for wildflowers, summer for swimming, fishing and beach walking.*

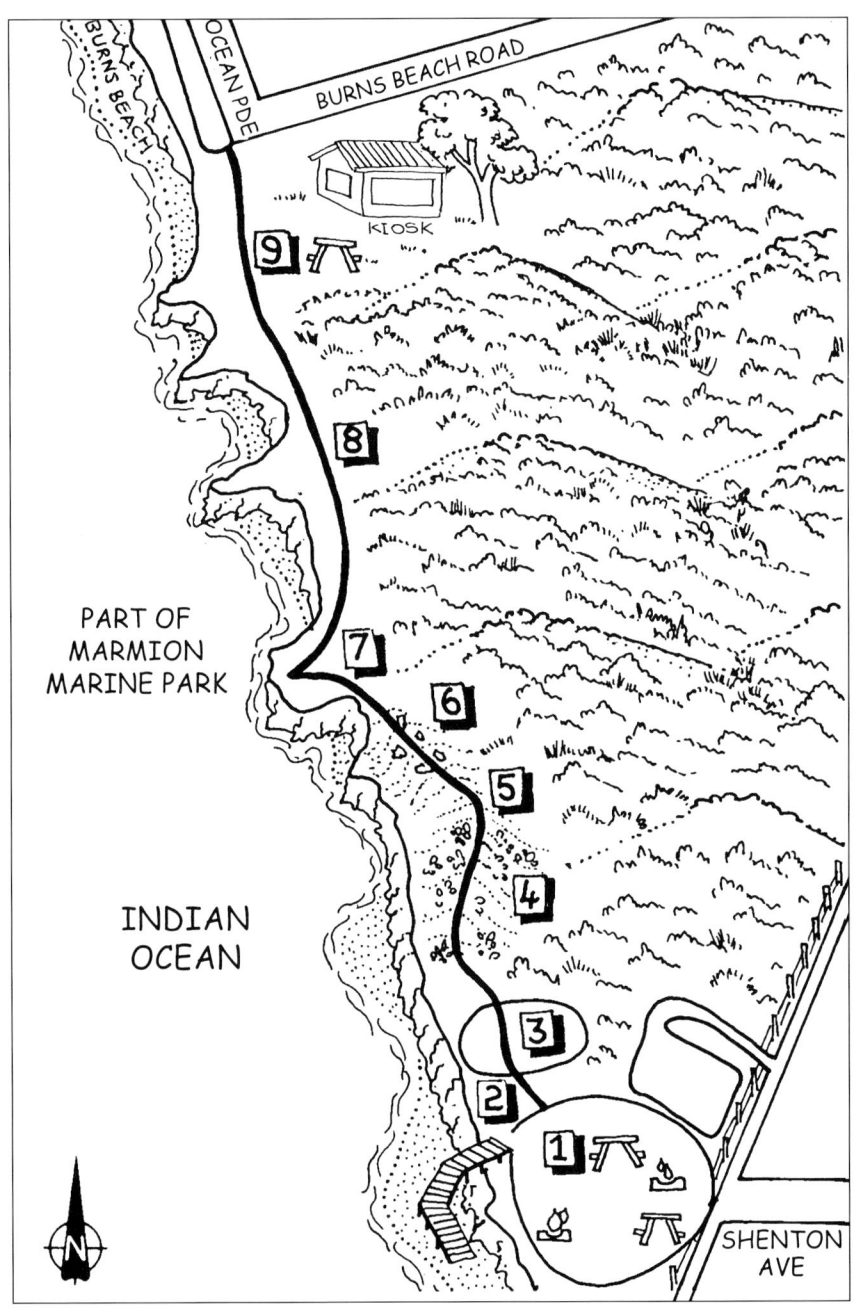

Iluka Foreshore Walktrail

17

Length: *4 km return.*
Class: *2.*
Walk time: *1 hour, 30 minutes.*

This pleasant clifftop walk leads from the Beaumaris Beach picnic area, along the foreshore reserve between Iluka and Burns Beach. An informal trail, stretching from Ocean Reef to Quinns Rocks, has existed for some years, but this section has been formalised and there are plans for a number of recreational features including a cafe. The walk takes you through typical dune vegetation and provides uninterrupted views of the ocean.

1   The trail leaves from the western end of Beaumaris Foreshore Park picnic area and heads north.
2   From here onwards you will see typical heath and dune vegetation, including smokebush, parrotbush, rushes, wattles, grevilleas and a variety of pea plants.
3   This is the site of a proposed cafe and sunken gardens.
4   Here you will see a number of other species including dune arctotheca, with its serrated paddle-shaped leaves, pigface and sea spinach.
5   From the top of this rise there are excellent views to the north and south, as well as inland across the foreshore reserve.
6   As you descend the northern slope of the rise, the limestone breaks through shallow surface soils.
7   The lookout point on the high limestone cliff provides excellent panoramic views.
8   There is access to a small sandy beach and a boardwalk is planned to make access easier. The vegetation near here is covered in dodder laurel, a parasitic orange coloured vine.
9   At Burns Beach there is a shop and cafe, carpark and safe bathing.

Linda, Sarah and Cole Armitage, Lynne Bradmore

Where is it? *26 km north-west of Perth at the western end of Shenton Avenue.*
Travelling time: *35 minutes from Perth via Marmion Avenue.*
Facilities: *BBQs, tables, shelter, carpark, cafe, shop.*
Best season: *All year.*

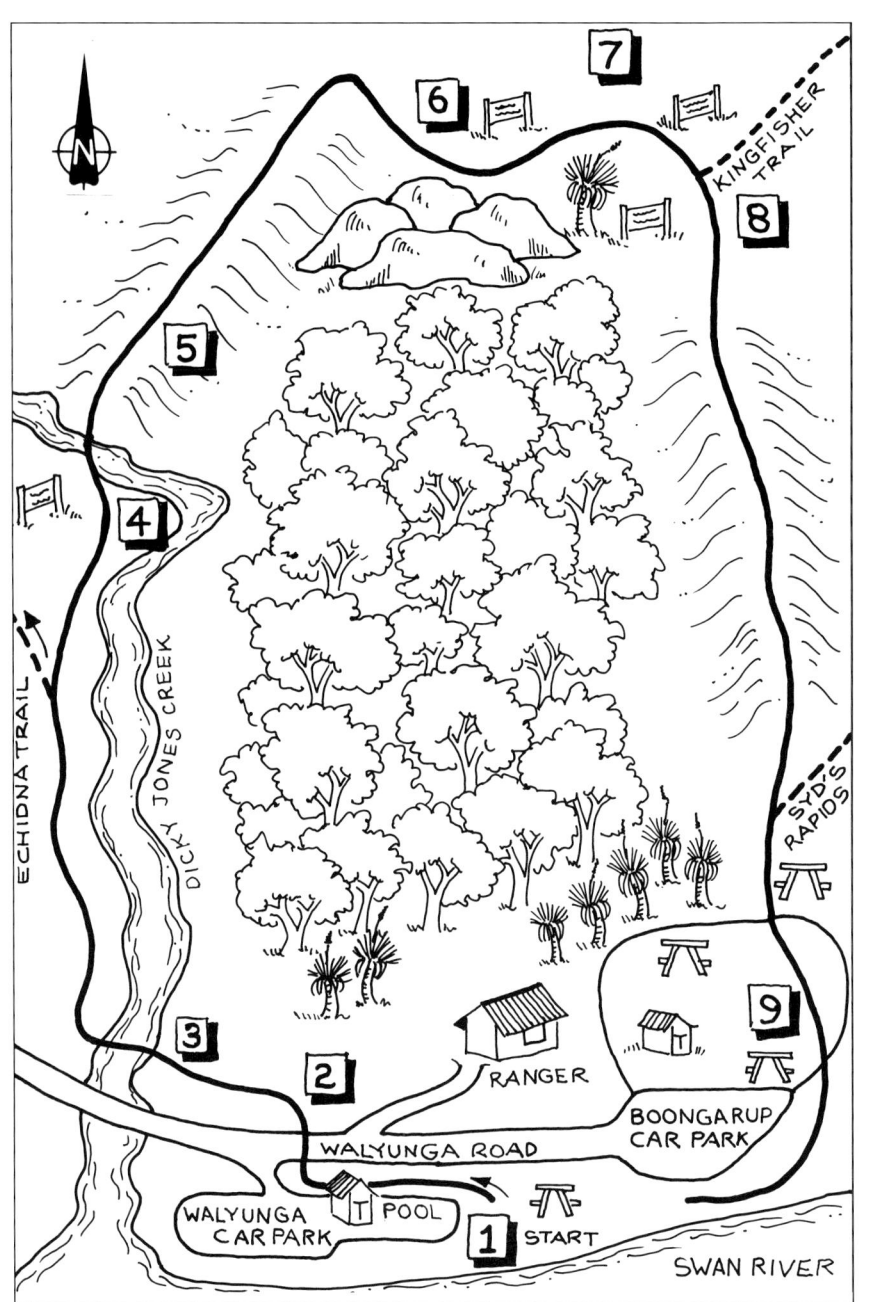

Kangaroo Trail **18**
Walyunga National Park ($)

Length: *4 km loop.*
Class: *4.*
Walk time: *2 hours.*

This is the shortest of three walktrails installed in 1992 with assistance from Rotary International. It offers a range of vegetation types and in spring it is possible to find delicate orchids beside the track. Eucalypts flower in the summer and honeyeaters are attracted to the blossoms.

1   Starting from the Walyunga Pool picnic area, follow the yellow kangaroo markers across the road.
2   This section is along an access track and moves steadily away from the road and into the woodland of wandoo and marri.
3   The trail crosses Dicky Jones Creek. There is an information panel giving details of an old dwelling that was in the area.
4   At the junction with the Echidna Trail, an information board provides details of trail options.
5   Crossing Dicky Jones Creek once again, the trail climbs uphill towards a granite outcrop.
6   There is an information panel about granite outcrops.
7   You soon reach a further information panel, this time about grasstrees.
8   Junction with the Kingfisher Trail. From here, the trail descends to the Boongarup Pool picnic area and the end of the Aboriginal Heritage Trail. Follow the Heritage Trail (in reverse) along the river's edge, which is lined with sheoaks and river gums, back to the Walyunga Pool picnic area.

Ross McGill, Steve Strachan

Where is it? *40 km north-east of Perth along Walyunga Road.*
Travelling time: *1 hour from Perth via the Great Northern Highway.*
Facilities: *BBQs, toilets, water, carparks at both picnic areas.*
On-site information: *Yellow kangaroo markers and information panels along the trail.*
Best season: *All year except hot summer days, spring for wildflowers.*

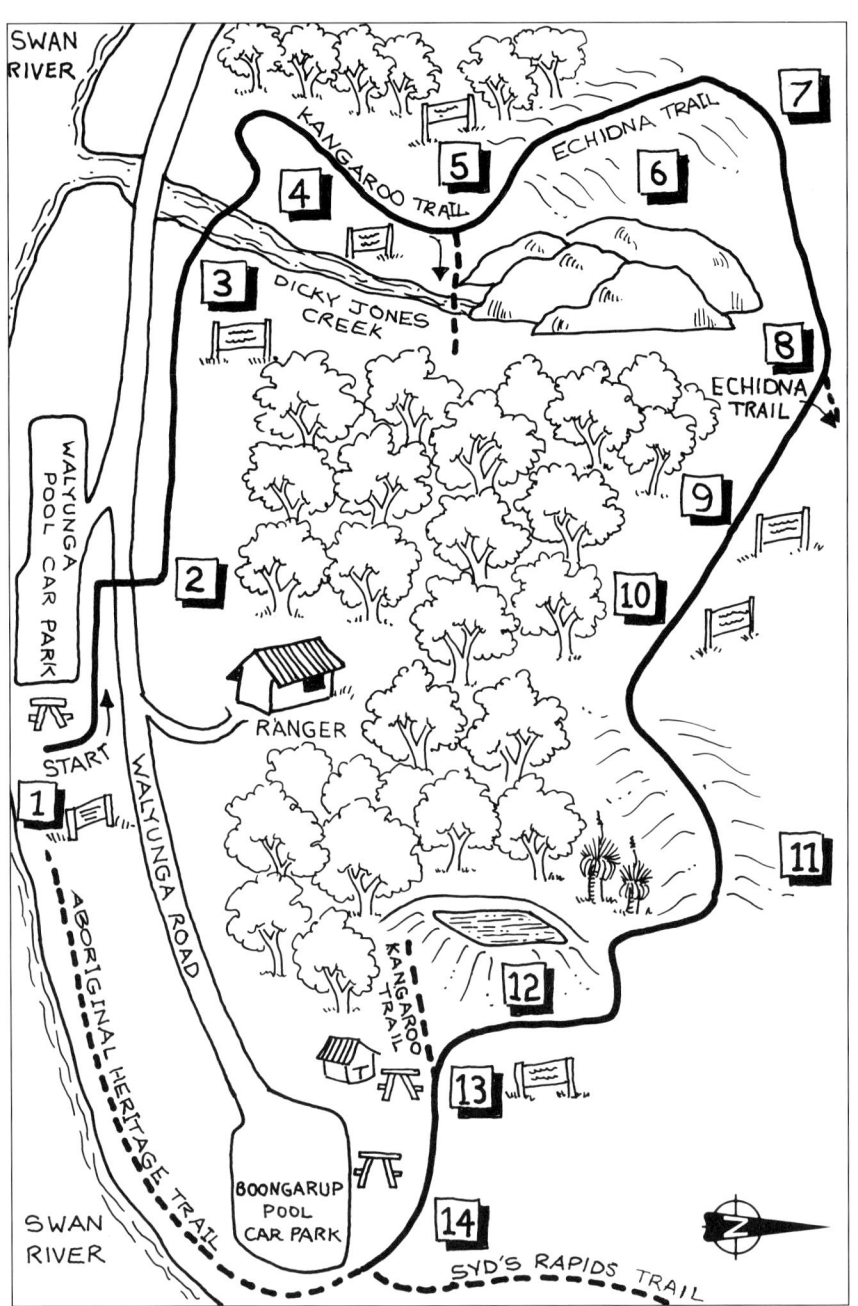

Kingfisher Trail

19

Walyunga National Park ($)

Length: *8.5 km loop.*
Class: *4.*
Walk time: *4 hours.*

The first half of this trail follows the Kangaroo and Echidna Trails before branching off. This trail was completed with assistance from Rotary International. The abundant wildlife and constant water supply in the park shows why Aboriginal people were so attracted to the area. Along the trail, you will notice large ant nests.

1   Starting from the Walyunga Pool picnic area, follow the Kangaroo Trail and cross the road near the toilet block.
2   This section is along an access track and moves steadily away from the road and into the woodland of wandoo and marri.
3   The trail crosses Dicky Jones Creek. An information panel provides details of an old dwelling that was in the area.
4   At the junction with the Echidna Trail, an information panel has details of trail options. Join the Echidna Trail and continue along it.
5   Another information panel outlines the habitats provided by wandoo trees.
6   At this point there are excellent views overlooking the valley and photographic opportunities.
7   The next vantage point has sweeping views over the Swan Coastal Plain.
8   The Kingfisher Trail leaves the Echidna Trail and heads south following blue kingfisher markers. An information panel provides details of trail options.
9   There is another information panel with details of wood borers found in wandoo trees.
10   A further information panel tells about the process by which fallen trees are broken down through rotting and returned to the soil.
11   This spot provides views across the valley.
12   The large dam to the right of the trail provides water for park toilets and gardens.
13   The Kingfisher Trail rejoins the shorter Kangaroo Trail and heads towards Boongarup Pool picnic area.
14   The trail joins the Aboriginal Heritage Trail and Syd's Rapids Trail. Follow the Aboriginal Heritage Trail along the river and back to the starting point at Walyunga Pool picnic area.

Ross McGill, Steve Strachan

Where is it? *40 km north-east of Perth along Walyunga Road.*
Travelling time: *1 hour from Perth via the Great Northern Highway.*
Facilities: *BBQs, toilets, water, carparks at both picnic areas.*
On-site information: *Trailhead sign, blue kingfisher markers and information panels along trail.*
Best season: *All year except hot summer days, spring for wildflowers.*

MUSK DUCK

The musk duck (*Biziura lobata*) is found on most waterways. It is usually seen floating motionless or kicking up great jets of water far from shore. This bird is perhaps the most prehistoric, unduck-like looking creature found in our parklands. It has blackish-brown plumage with numerous fine lines of light brown and floats very low in the water. An unusual leathery bag hangs under the chin of mature males.

During the breeding season, male musk ducks have an intense odour emanating from their oil or preen gland, which is situated on the birds' rumps. Courting birds stage a remarkable display by blowing out cheeks and neck, inflating their chin bag, spreading their spiny tail feathers over their back, throwing water and giving out a piercing, most unduck-like whistle with each kick.

As with other waterfowl, water levels determine breeding; so from the first rains in March through to September you are likely to see these individuals perform.

Musk ducks feed entirely by diving and can remain submerged for up to a minute as they dive deep in search of aquatic insects, mussels, snails, crustaceans and frogs. The birds are entirely aquatic and almost helpless on land. To escape detection they sink into the water, leaving only their eyes and nostrils exposed.

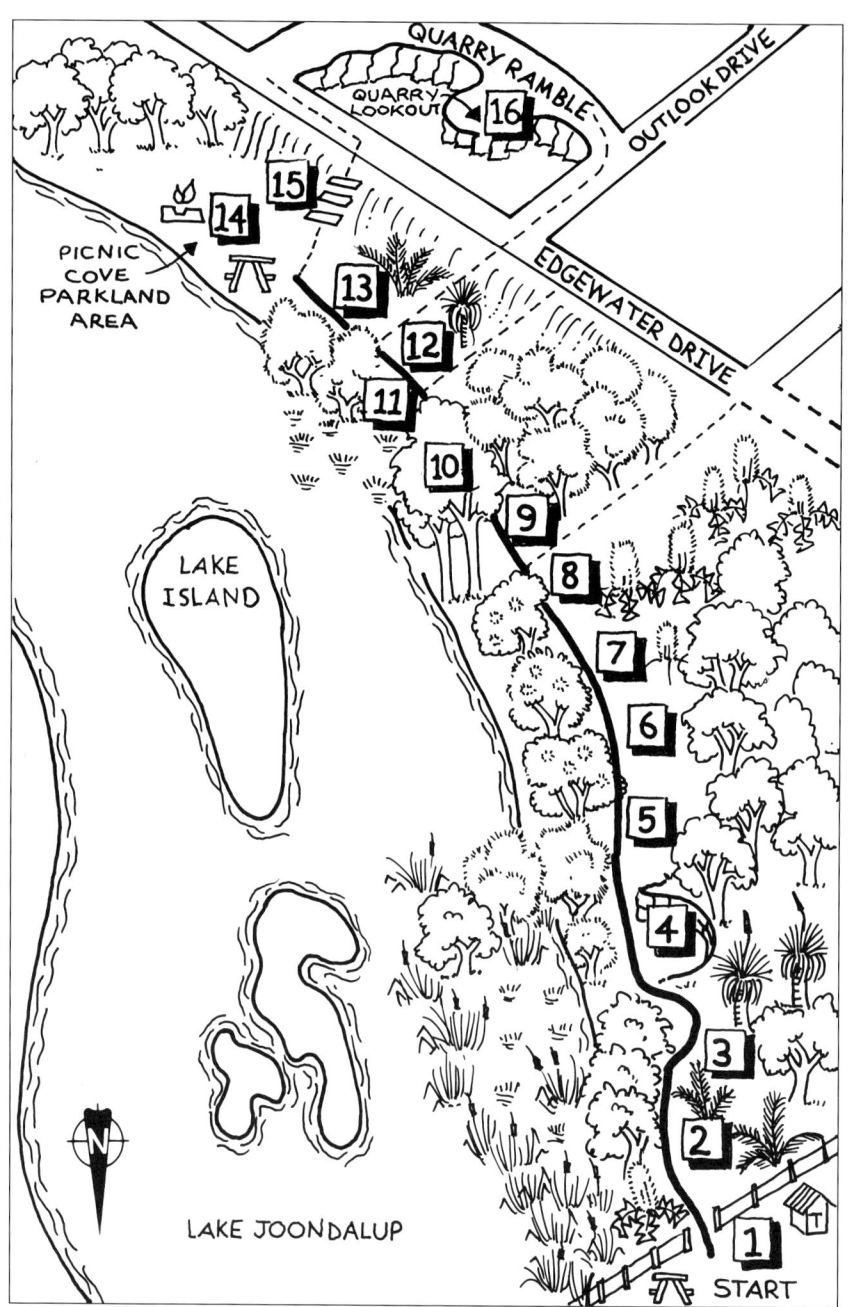

Lake Joondalup Nature Trail

20

Neil Hawkins Park, Yellagonga Regional Park

Length: 5 km return.
Class: 2.
Walk time: 2 hours.

This nature trail takes you along a limestone track south from Neil Hawkins Park by the edge of Lake Joondalup. It features paperbarks and rushes on the lake's edge and banksia-marri woodland in the drier areas to the west of the track. There is a gradual, but interesting change in vegetation types along the trail, which ends in a formal grassed area with basic picnic facilities by the lake's edge. There is an optional one kilometre loop to Quarry Lookout, which gives panoramic views across the entire lake.

1 Follow the limestone track at the south end of Neil Hawkins Park, where there are banksias and wattles.
2 Paperbarks and rushes dominate the lake edge on the left of the trail, while banksias, zamias (*Macrozamia reidlei*), eucalypts and parrotbush (*Dryandra sessilis*) grow on the right. The trail is shaded by a canopy of trees.
3 Two large grasstrees can be seen at the bend. The canopy begins to thin.
4 A boardwalk leads to an observation platform at the lake's edge.
5 Here, the paperbarks extend into swampy areas on both sides of the trail.
6 Groves of golden wattles form a canopy over the trail.
7 A large old banksia extends above the pathway.
8 To the right, a sand track leads up through the woodland to Edgewater Road.
9 Wattles and melaleucas form a canopy over the trail.
10 Tall gums tower above the paperbarks on the left.
11 Here the canopy opens out to a swampy area with paperbarks on the left, wattles on the right and banksias on the far right.
12 Another sand track leads up to Edgewater Road.
13 The trail opens out to a paddock with zamias and occasional trees.
14 There is a picnic area with a wood barbecue. From here, you can retrace your steps or continue to Quarry Lookout.
15 Climb the steps and head south along the footpath. Cross Edgewater Road into Quarry Ramble and walk uphill on the right of the road.

16 Quarry Lookout provides magnificent panoramic views over the entire lake. From here, continue along Quarry Ramble, turn right into Outlook Drive then retrace your steps along the trail to Neil Hawkins Park.

David Gough, Therese Jones

Where is it? *Neil Hawkins Park, Boas Avenue, Joondalup, 25 km north of Perth.*
Travelling time: *40 minutes via the Mitchell Freeway and Joondalup Drive. You can also travel by train to Joondalup and walk through Central Park to Neil Hawkins Park.*
Facilities: *BBQs, picnic tables, playground, toilets, carpark, large grassy area, bird observation platform.*
Best season: *All year.*

BANKSIA WOODLANDS

BULL BANKSIA

There are many species of banksia in WA, ranging from low-lying shrubs to large trees, and at least one species is in flower at any time of the year. The attractive flowers, clustered together in cylindrical, conical, dome-shaped or spherical heads, attract and support a wide range of insects, birds and mammals.

Six species of banksia occur as trees on the Swan Coastal Plain. They generally form a woodland with a rich understorey of zamias, grasstrees, native shrubs, delicate orchids and a host of other wildflowers.

Firewood banksia (*Banksia menziesii*) has toothed leaves and yellow and pinkish-orange flowering spikes. Candle banksia (*B. attenuata*) has a narrow cylindrical cone of yellow flowers and narrow, slightly serrated leaves. The orange-flowered acorn banksia (*B. prionotes*) occurs on pockets of yellow soil. It can be found in Kings Park and on similar soils further north. The bull banksia (*B. grandis*) has leaves up to 40 centimetres long and occurs on grey sand, often with sheoaks. Holly-leaf banksia (*B. ilicifolia*) is a graceful tree superficially like candle banksia, but growing in even wetter ground around the perimeter of swamps and lakes. Its branches are long and erect with dark green holly-like leaves and flowers of cream and pink in a dome-shaped head.

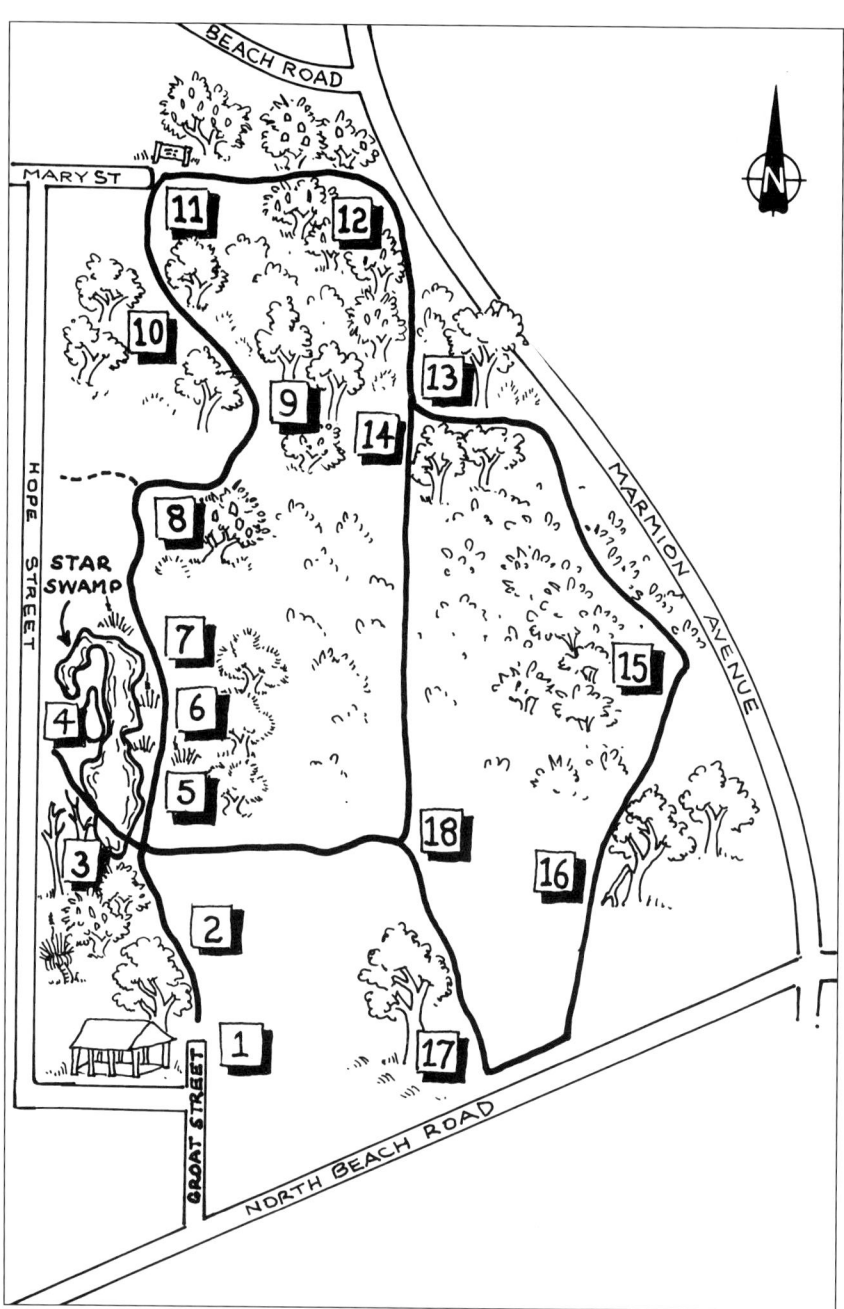

Star Swamp Trail

21

Star Swamp Bushland Reserve

Length: *4 km loop.*
Class: *2 (accessible by wheelchair, except after heavy rain).*
Walk time: *1 hour, 30 minutes.*

Star Swamp Bushland Reserve is a 100 hectare nature reserve. The walk incorporates the Star Swamp Heritage Trail and native bushland just west of Marmion Avenue, passing through every vegetation type in the reserve. The area sustains a rich diversity of plant and animal life in tranquil settings, and the walk offers opportunities for birdwatching and picnicking.

1   Starting at the Groat Street entrance, there is a large shelter built by Rotary International and a Heritage Trail sign. A very large, old tuart tree marks the start of banksia-sheoak woodland with orchids, pimelias and acacias.
2   To the left of the trail there are two firewood banksias. There are also grasstrees and native buttercups (*Hibbertia hypericifolia*).
3   Sacred kingfishers, galahs and 'twenty-eight' parrots nest in the dead tuarts on the left.
4   From here to point 8, there is typical swamp-lake vegetation of paperbarks, white spray (*Logania* sp.), rare bitter bush (*Adriana* sp.), basket bush (*Spyridium* sp.), reeds and sedges. Bird life includes white-faced herons, ibises, ducks and nesting night herons. Many frogs can be heard calling during winter and early spring.
5   In the mid-1800s, cattle were driven down the Coastal Stock Route from Dongara to Fremantle. Star Swamp was one of many watering places en route. Original posts of an old stockyard can still be seen on the northern side of the swamp.
6   The swamp was also a frequent watering hole for dairy cattle from the local Bettles Dairy, which closed in 1915.
7   Marl is a clay-like sediment that was used to seal limestone roads constructed in 1919 as part of the first housing subdivision. It was sometimes quarried from the swamp and evidence of this can be seen when the water level is low.
8   To the right of the trail is the first of the bull banksias (*Banksia grandis*) and a large spreading tuart tree with a shrubland of prickly moses (*Acacia pulchella*), hairy grevilleas (*Grevillea vestita*), dwarf sheoaks (*Allocasuarina humilis*), stinkwood (*Jacksonia* sp.) and grasstrees. If you take the right fork in the track, you will pass through a good stand of harsh hakea (*Hakea prostrata*), native wisteria (*Hardenbergia* sp.), with its bright blue flowers, and jarrah trees.

9   This section of track is all that is left of a major track that ran through the bushland in a south-easterly direction from Mary Street to North Beach Road. Here, the vegetation changes to woodland of tuart, jarrah and banksia.

10   The vegetation changes again, this time to marri woodland. In late winter, the white flowers of old man's beard (*Clematis pubescens*) appear.

11   Up ahead is the Mary Street entrance with a Heritage Trail sign and map. This marks the end of the Heritage Trail and you should now turn right. There is a large bull banksia beside the reserve sign and panoramic views to Duncraig.

12   Coming up to Marmion Avenue there is a large stand of acorn banksia (*B. prionotes*) on the left. See if you can spot candle banksia (*B. attenuata*) and the white star flowers of wedding bush (*Ricinocarpos glaucus*) on your right.

13   Several dead tuart trees on the left are used by corellas, galahs and 'twenty-eight' parrots for nesting. Looking right you can see the old water tower, now a museum, on Mount Flora. In late winter, the understorey of this tuart-banksia woodland is a sea of yellow prickly moses, with occasional scarlet runner (*Kennedia prostrata*) and native violet (*Hybanthus calycinus*).

14   The Observation City Hotel can be seen straight ahead. The vegetation opens up to a heathland of parrotbush (*Dryandra sessilis*), native buttercup, one-sided bottlebrush (*Calothamnus quadrifidus*) and summer-scented wattle (*Acacia rostellifera*). White-cheeked honeyeaters can be seen on the parrotbush. Those wanting to stay on the limestone track (such as wheelchair users) should cut through to point 17 on the map, otherwise follow the sand track to the left.

15   The sand track passes a large stand (about one hectare) of hairy grevillea, with masses of pink and white flowers in late winter.

16   On the left is a tuart tree with a fallen branch. This is a good spot to look for blue fairy orchids in July and August.

17   The large tuart tree on the left marks a limestone outcrop with cockie's tongues (*Templetonia retusa*) and truncate wattle (*Acacia truncata*), which together give a display of bright red and yellow flowers.

18   Meeting up with the limestone track, follow the Heritage Trail sign down the track through a woodland of tuart, jarrah, banksia and sheoak to point 2 on the map. Here you have a choice: you may return to the start at Groat Street or proceed to the lawned area in Hope Street (point 4 on the map) and have a picnic overlooking the lake and its waterbirds.

David Pike, Daniel Rajah

Where is it? *15 km north-west of Perth. Access is from Groat Street via Marmion Avenue, North Beach Road.*
Travelling time: *25 minutes.*
Facilities: *None.*
On-site information: *Trailhead sign, interpretive signs along Heritage Trail section only.*
Best season: *All year. Spring for wildflowers.*

FROGS

Frogs are amphibians. They begin life as tadpoles before eventually becoming four-legged, air-breathing adults.

Two families of frogs occur around Perth: tree frogs and ground frogs.

Tree frogs are large, with mottled brown or green colouring, and have circular discs on their toes. The bull frog (*Litoria moorei*) is between five and seven centimetres long and may have warty skin. The slender tree frog (*L. adelaidensis*), however, is between three and five centimetres long, smoother and wholly brown or green, except for a stripe along the body and red spots on the backs of the thighs. Both species live around wetlands and lay large masses of eggs, which are attached to vegetation at water level during spring.

Ground frogs have no circular discs on their toes and generally have warty skins. Some are only two or three centimetres long, while some lay eggs in water and others in burrows. The male moaning frog (*Heleioporus eyrei*) will construct a burrow and call the female to him.

All frogs are carnivorous. Small frogs have a predominantly insectivorous diet, but they also eat snails, earthworms and spiders. Larger frogs may eat scorpions, centipedes, lizards and even smaller frogs!

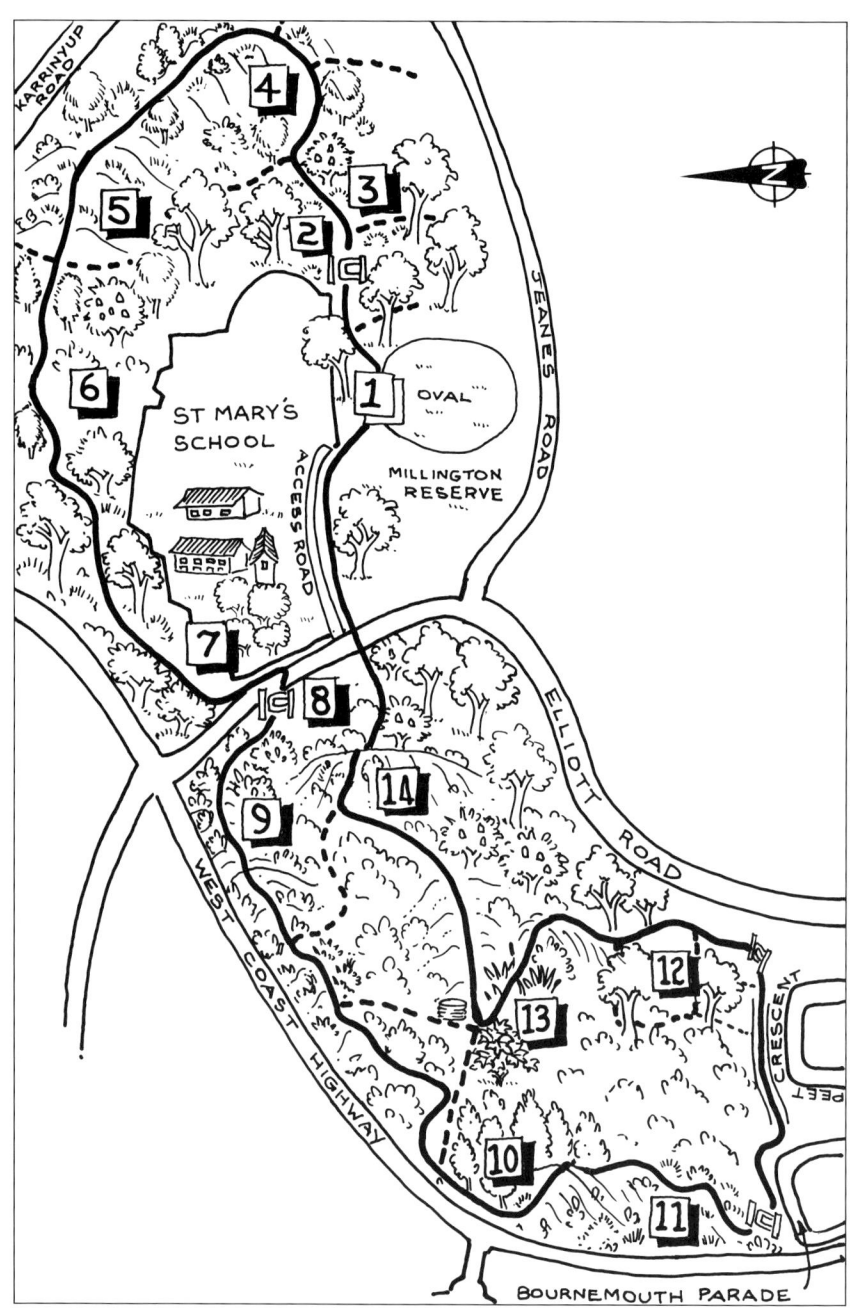

Trigg Bushland Trail

22

Trigg Bushland Reserve

Length: *5 km loop.*
Class: *3.*
Walk time: *2 hours.*

This figure-of-eight trail takes you through one of the most important, but least well-known areas of natural coastal vegetation found anywhere in metropolitan Perth. It features views of the ocean and Rottnest Island, remnant groves of Rottnest cypress (*Callitris preissii*) and tuart (*Eucalyptus gomphocephala*) forest, abundant bird life and masses of spring wildflowers.

1   Starting from Millington Reserve, just south of St Mary's School, walk along the access road and across the reserve to the edge of the bushland, keeping the school's cyclone fence to your left. You will pass some large tuart trees.
2   Enter the bushland through a turnstile. This is an open woodland of tuart with some acorn banksia (*Banksia prionotes*). The understorey is mostly one-sided bottlebrush and dune moses, with some clematis and native wisteria. Proceed east on a limestone track.
3   Take the second left fork. There are dune sheoaks nearby. At the next fork turn right. Notice the replantings of Rottnest cypress. Carry on up the slope of the dune, keeping to the limestone track.
4   Keep left at the next junction. Here, you are on the rim of one of the easternmost sand dunes of a major dune blowout system. The ocean is visible to the west and Rottnest Island will soon be visible on the horizon. Quandong (*Santalum acuminatum*), parrotbush, one-sided bottlebrush and coast daisy bush, with its blue leaves, grow here.
5   Continue west along the ridgeline through dune sheoaks and cross another track. Corkybark (*Gyrostemon ramulosus*), more often found in dry inland areas, and dune sheoak grow on the northern slope. On your left, you will pass a twisted specimen of corkybark.
6   Turn left at the next junction, then almost immediately turn right. This section passes between the perimeter fence of the school and the West Coast Highway.
7   You are now outside the bushland. Turn left and walk towards the school's main entrance and cross Elliott Road to the turnstile.
8   Follow the limestone track past summer-scented wattle (*Acacia rostellifera*) and thickets of quandongs to a grove of tuarts in a sheltered area. The track climbs

slowly (ignore the steep track on your left). You are now climbing one of the inner dunes of the dune blowout system.

9 At the crest, there is a clear view of the ocean near Trigg Beach with Rottnest Island on the horizon. The track descends past a thicket of parrotbush, which is very popular with birds such as white-cheeked honeyeaters. Turn right at the junction.

10 The track descends before curving away from the sea and climbing to a crest, with Observation City Hotel visible behind dunes supporting groves of Rottnest cypress. Other cypress are close by on the ridgetop. It's thought that Rottnest cypress once covered extensive areas of the Swan Coastal Plain.

11 Before passing through the Bournemouth Parade turnstile, near West Coast Highway, you can see vegetation typical of coastal shrubland: fanflowers, spinifex and coastal sword sedge (*Lepidosperma gladiatum*). From here, you may decide to cross the highway to visit the beach before continuing your walk. Follow Bournemouth Parade inland and, around the corner, take the public footpath through to Peet Crescent and on to Elliott Road. Turn left and re-enter the bushland at the turnstile.

12 Turn right and follow the limestone track downhill, ignoring the left hand track at the bottom of the slope. Here, there is a sheltered area of tuarts, Rottnest cypress and summer-scented wattle. The track climbs steeply, then descends through more wattle and patches of sword sedge.

13 Fig trees, water tanks and foundations mark the site of a house built in the 1930s as part of an unsuccessful subdivision. Turn right at the track junction.

14 After climbing through more wattle, turn right again at the next junction. This leads over the crest of a dune and descends to Elliott Road, opposite the access road to Millington Reserve.

Steve Tulip, Daniel Rajah

Where is it? *12 km north-west of Perth.*
Travelling time: *30 minutes via Karrinyup Road and Marmion Avenue.*
Facilities: *Offroad parking adjacent to Millington Reserve, Elliott Road.*
On-site information: *Maps of bushland at Bournemouth Road and Elliott Road entrances.*
Best season: *All year, especially spring for wildflowers. Early mornings and evenings are best in warmer months.*

RATS AND MICE

BUSH RAT

Rodents (rats and mice) are usually thought of as those 'uglies' that were introduced to Australia by Europeans. In fact, about five to ten million years ago, some species entered Australia from New Guinea and continued on an evolutionary course to occupy habitats from rainforest to deserts. These animals now have differing appearances, as their environments have dictated physical change.

About a million years ago a new group arrived. These have also found diverse habitats but they still resemble typical Asian rats.

There are now 58 species of native rodents, ranging from the beaver-like water-rat (*Hydromys chrysogaster*) and the spinifex hopping-mouse (*Notomys alexis*) to the bush rat (*Rattus fuscipes*).

The domestic rats and mice that we often see in our towns and cities were introduced by Europeans some 200 years ago and have now spread out into natural habitats across much of the continent.

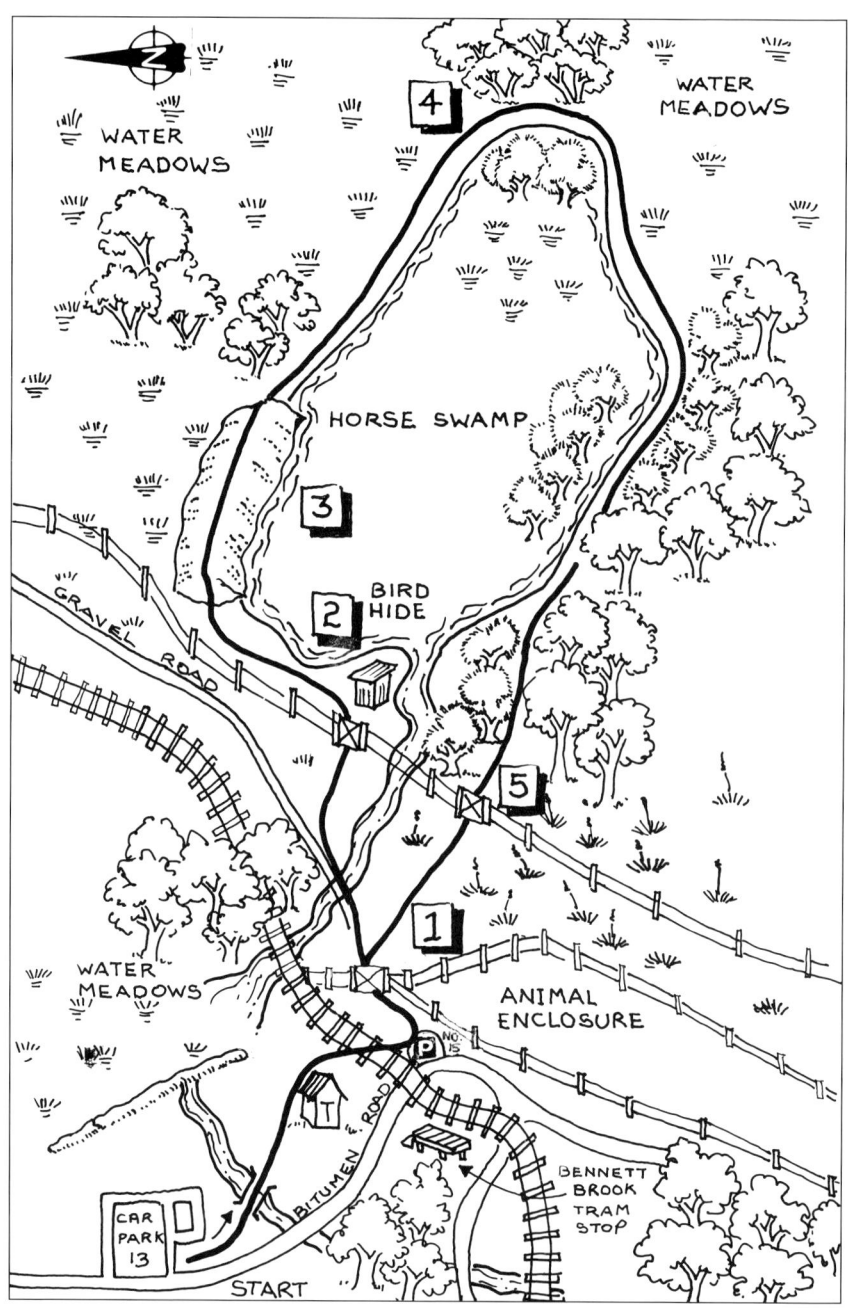

WATER MEADOWS

WATER MEADOWS

4

HORSE SWAMP

3

2 BIRD HIDE

GRAVEL ROAD

5

1

WATER MEADOWS

ANIMAL ENCLOSURE

BITUMEN ROAD

CAR PARK 13

BENNETT BROOK TRAM STOP

START

Werillyiup Walktrail   **23**

Whiteman Park ($)

Length: *3 km loop.*
Class: *3.*
Walk time: *50 minutes.*

'Werillyiup' means 'a swampy place' in the local Aboriginal language. The walktrail takes you around Horse Swamp, named by the early settlers because escaped horses were often found grazing there. From December to June the swamp is usually dry. After the rains in May/June, the swamp fills and surrounding meadows become waterlogged. Many birds can be seen here in winter, spring and early summer. It is common to see several black swans at this time, as at least two pairs nest and produce offspring each year. The trail begins at Car Park 13 on the western side of Mussel Pool, but can also be joined at Car Park 15 near the Animal Enclosure.

1   About 120 metres from the start, the trail passes through a gate and then splits. Follow the left hand branch along the gravel road, across the stream at the culvert then turn to the right.
2   Soon after passing through the next gate, a track to the right leads to the bird hide (at trail marker 'A'), from which you can often see coots and red-legged stilts.
3   From the dam wall ('B') there are good views along the length of the swamp. Black swans and ibises can often be seen.
4   At the eastern end of the swamp ('C') a large grove of flooded gums (*Eucalyptus rudis*) is used by grey kangaroos to shelter from the heat. Stout paperbarks (*Melaleuca preissiana*) are scattered around the drier parts of the swamp, while freshwater paperbarks (*M. rhaphiophylla*) often stand in the water. A grove of these at trail marker 'D' is favoured by purple swamphens and coots for nesting.
5   The trail leaves the swamp and cuts through a thicket of paperbarks, stinkwood and marri. It passes through a gate, then continues through a large area of grasstrees (*Xanthorrhoea brunonis*), at point 'E', which differ from the more common grasstree in not having a trunk above the ground.

Dave Bright and other Whiteman Park staff

Where is it? *18 km north of Perth. Entrance off Lord Street, West Swan.*
Travelling time: *25 minutes from Perth.*
Facilities: *BBQs, picnic areas, toilets, water, carpark, restaurant.*
On-site information: *Trailhead sign, blue topped poles, interpretive signs.*
Best season: *Winter, spring, early summer.*

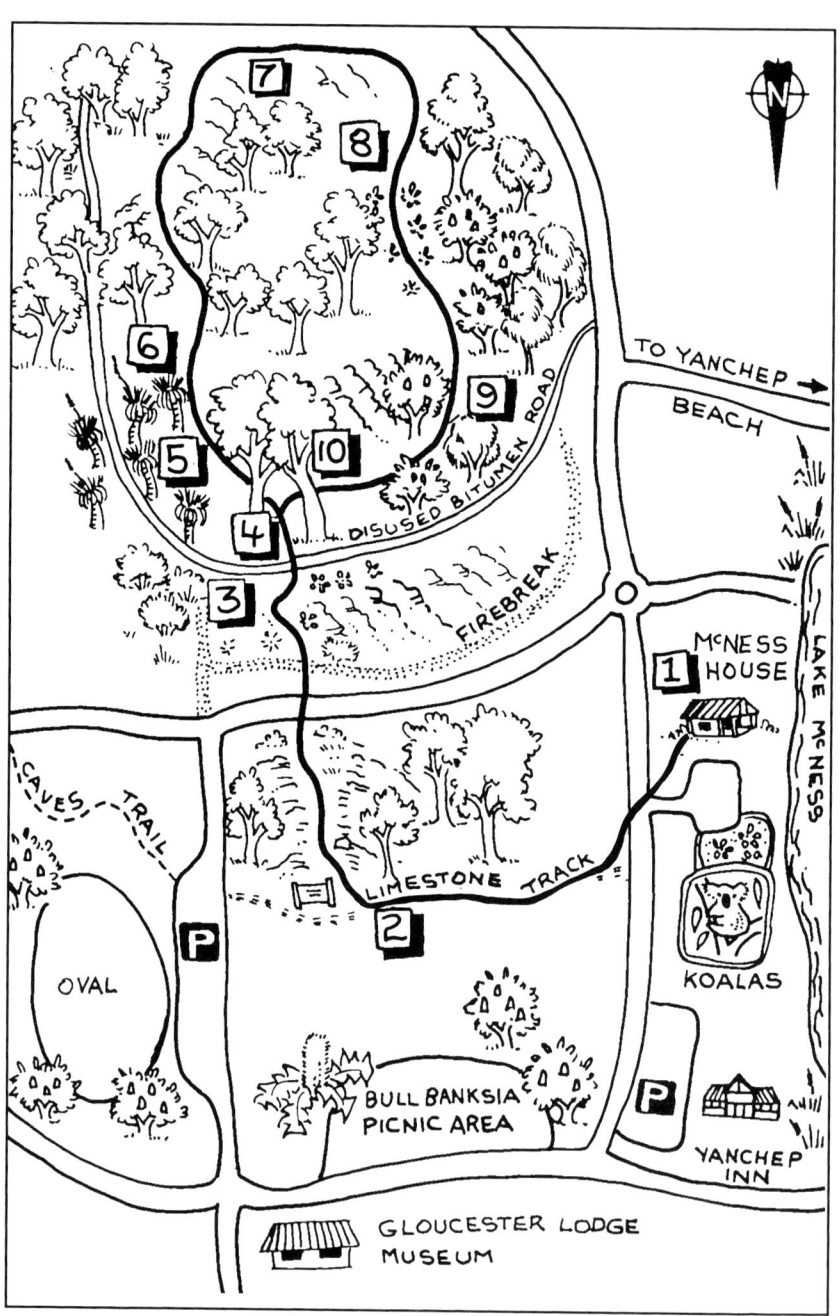

Woodlands Walktrail

24

Yanchep National Park ($)

Length: *2.6 km.*
Class: *3. Some rocky and uneven surfaces.*
Walk time: *1 hour.*

This is a peaceful stroll through the woodlands in Yanchep National Park. Please take care as some sections are rocky.

1   Begin at McNess Visitor Centre. Follow the paved pathway until the trail takes a right turn across the road and onto a limestone track. Take care crossing the road.
2   The trail splits from the other trails to the right. Wind along a limestone ridge down a gentle slope to the road. Again, take care when crossing the road.
3   Head up a small rocky ridge, with views into surrounding valleys. Many low heath plants, including spider net grevilleas and bottlebrush, bloom here in spring.
4   Continue to a sharp left turn and walk down to an old bitumen road. Cross the road and enter the woodlands through a gateway of two magnificent tuart (*Eucalyptus gomphocephala*) trees on either side of the trail.
5   Follow the trail on your left to a grove of grasstrees or balgas. During the warmer months be careful not to startle the western grey kangaroos that use the skirts of the balga to shelter from the midday sun. Balgas only grow about 1.5 centimetres each year, so a 1.5 metre balga would be about 100 years old!
6   The trail winds around a rocky ridge, down into a woodland of coastal jarrah and marri. Due to extensive clearing, there are only a few pockets of these mixed woodlands left on the Swan Coastal Plain.
7   Head through the woodland to an isolated paperbark thicket in a small wetland.
8   Follow the trail up a rocky limestone ridge. From August to October, this area is carpeted by wildflowers such as native buttercups, red kangaroo paws, orange catspaws and snakebush (mauve flowers with dark pink spots).
9   The trail moves away from the ridge and into a woodland of banksias and sheoaks.
10 Continue back to the two large tuart trees. Turn left, cross the road and follow the markers back to the start. Take care when crossing roads.

Therese Jones

Where is it? *Yanchep National Park, 51 km north of Perth on Wanneroo Road.*
Travelling time: *1 hour from Perth.*
Facilities: *BBQs, picnic shelters and toilets in nearby picnic areas.*
Best season: *Spring, winter and autumn.*

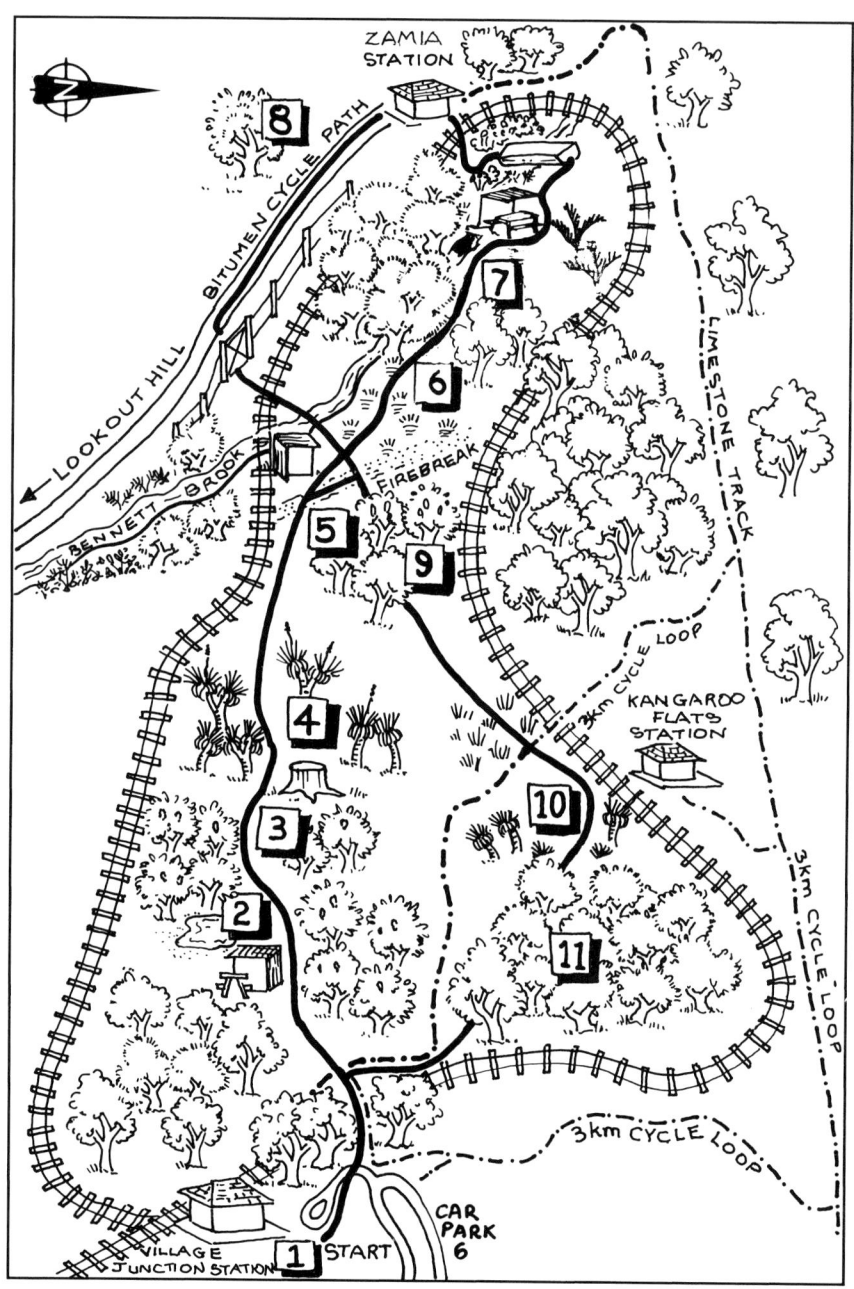

ZAMIA STATION

LOOKOUT HILL

BITUMEN CYCLE PATH

BENNETT BROOK

FIREBREAK

LIMESTONE TRACK

3km CYCLE LOOP

KANGAROO FLATS STATION

3km CYCLE LOOP

3km CYCLE LOOP

CAR PARK 6

VILLAGE JUNCTION STATION

1 START

2

3

4

5

6

7

8

9

10

11

Wunanga Walktrail

25

Whiteman Park ($)

Length: *4.3 km figure of eight loop.*
Class: *3.*
Walk time: *1 hour, 40 minutes.*

In the local Aboriginal language, 'Wunanga' means 'quiet' or 'peaceful'. The walktrail meanders through an area of bushland that is encircled by the park's railway system and traverses a variety of plant habitats. A brochure with more information about this walktrail is available from the information centre.

1   The trail starts at Village Junction Station and heads north-west along the edge of the bitumen road, across the road at the western end of Car Park 6, through a grove of marris (*Corymbia calophylla*) and left onto a limestone track.

2   At the T-junction, the trail leaves the limestone track and heads into open woodland. There is a woodland of marri and paperbark to the left, with woodland of banksia ('A') and pricklybark to the right. After about 500 metres, the trail passes a shelter, followed by a small dam (trail marker 'B').

3   A bit further on, the trail climbs slightly through a mixed banksia woodland. Trail marker 'C' marks a candle banksia (*B. attenuata*), 'D' is a holly-leaf banksia (*Banksia ilicifolia*) and 'E' is the more common firewood banksia (*B. menziesii*).

4   By the side of the trail is an old jarrah stump blackened by many bushfires and aged around 200 at the time it fell. To the left ('H'), several younger jarrah stems can be seen growing out of an old lignotuber, the original tree having been killed by a bushfire several years ago.

5   The trail then passes through a grove of grasstrees or balgas (*Xanthorrhoea preissii*), some of which have trunks of up to three metres high and multiple crowns. Soon afterwards, the trail reaches a firebreak. You are now just over a kilometre from the start. Turn right along the firebreak, then right again after about 100 metres to follow the shorter trail with orange-topped posts.

6   The yellow trail continues to a small winter-wet swamp ('K') with several large paperbarks (*Melaleuca preissiana*). The wetland sedge *Cyathochaeta teretifolia* ('L'). The largest known stand of this species in the world occurs in Whiteman Park. As the trail opens out, you will see, over to the left, some paperbarks with an understorey of bracken fern (*Pteridium esculentum*) marking the line of Bennett Brook. Although *esculentum* means 'edible', bracken is poisonous when consumed raw and in large quantities.

7 Near the second shelter is an area of zamias ('M') or cycads (*Macrozamia reidlei*). Shortly thereafter, the trail crosses Bennett Brook by means of a fallen paperbark log, then goes through a dense patch of bracken fern ('N').

8 After passing Zamia Station, follow the bitumen cycle path for 150 metres past a WA Christmas tree (*Nuytsia floribunda*), at trail point 'Q'. This area, known as the Santa Maria paddocks, was grazed by cattle until the mid-1990s. Turn left through the gate, along an old blue metal surfaced firebreak, across the railway track and back across Bennett Brook. Small pools of water, with tadpoles in spring, lie on either side of the culvert ('S'). The trail crossroad is marked 'T'. Follow the yellowish-orange sighting poles through beautiful woodland, rich in a variety of wildflowers, including pink summer starflower (*Calytrix fraseri*), which blooms during spring and summer.

9 For the next 500 metres, the trail winds through a beautiful patch of banksia-jarrah-marri woodland that is rich in a variety of wildflowers, particularly in spring. Trail marker 'U' marks a bull banksia (*B. grandis*). Masses of cowslip orchids (*Caladenia flava*) can be seen in this area during September.

10 As the trail leaves the trees, it passes through an area of low, tufty sedge-like plants ('V'). These are *Phlebocarya ciliata*, which belong to the same family as kangaroo paws. The trail crosses a limestone track ('three kilometre loop') then passes through a large clump of grasstrees. Two different species occur here. Balga (*Xanthorrhoea preissii*) produces a trunk as it ages. Brown's grasstree (*Xanthorrhoea brunonis*) only has an underground stem and often branches, resulting in the formation of clumps. Kangaroo Flats Station can be seen to the left ('W').

11 The next 200 metres of trail passes through open woodland of stout paperbarks or modongs (*Melaleuca preissiana*) at trail point 'X', before joining the limestone track. After a short distance, a very large marri ('Z') appears to the left. The trail finishes back at Village Junction Station.

Dave Bright and Jo Wallace

Where is it? *18 km north of Perth. Entrance off Lord Street, West Swan.*
Travelling time: *25 minutes from Perth.*
Facilities: *Picnic shelters. BBQs, carpark, toilets, restaurant in the village.*
On-site information: *Trailhead sign, yellow-topped posts along route.*
Best season: *All year, spring for wildflowers.*

SNAKES

When out walking during warm weather, around the block or through local parks or wetlands, you may cross paths with a snake. There is, however, no need to panic. The fact that wildlife exists on these walks makes them educational and fulfilling. The truth is, snakes are more afraid of you and if you walk normally and boldly, most will sense your approach and move off.

The more commonly occurring venomous snakes found in the Perth Outdoors area are the front-fanged dugite and tiger snakes.

The dugite (*Pseudonaja affinis*) is olive brown or dark brown and may have odd black spots. This snake is fond of mice.

The western tiger snake (*Notechis scutatus occidentalis*) is an aggressive and dangerous reptile. It can be recognised by its rather stout form, broad head and dark blackish colour, with or without a large number of pale yellowish-orange cross bands. The undersurface is usually pale yellowish-orange. It prefers damp swampy situations where frogs abound and, at times, takes small lizards, mammals and birds.

If you are unlucky enough to be bitten by a snake, information on the treatment of snake bites is given in the 'Walking Safely' section at the front of this book.

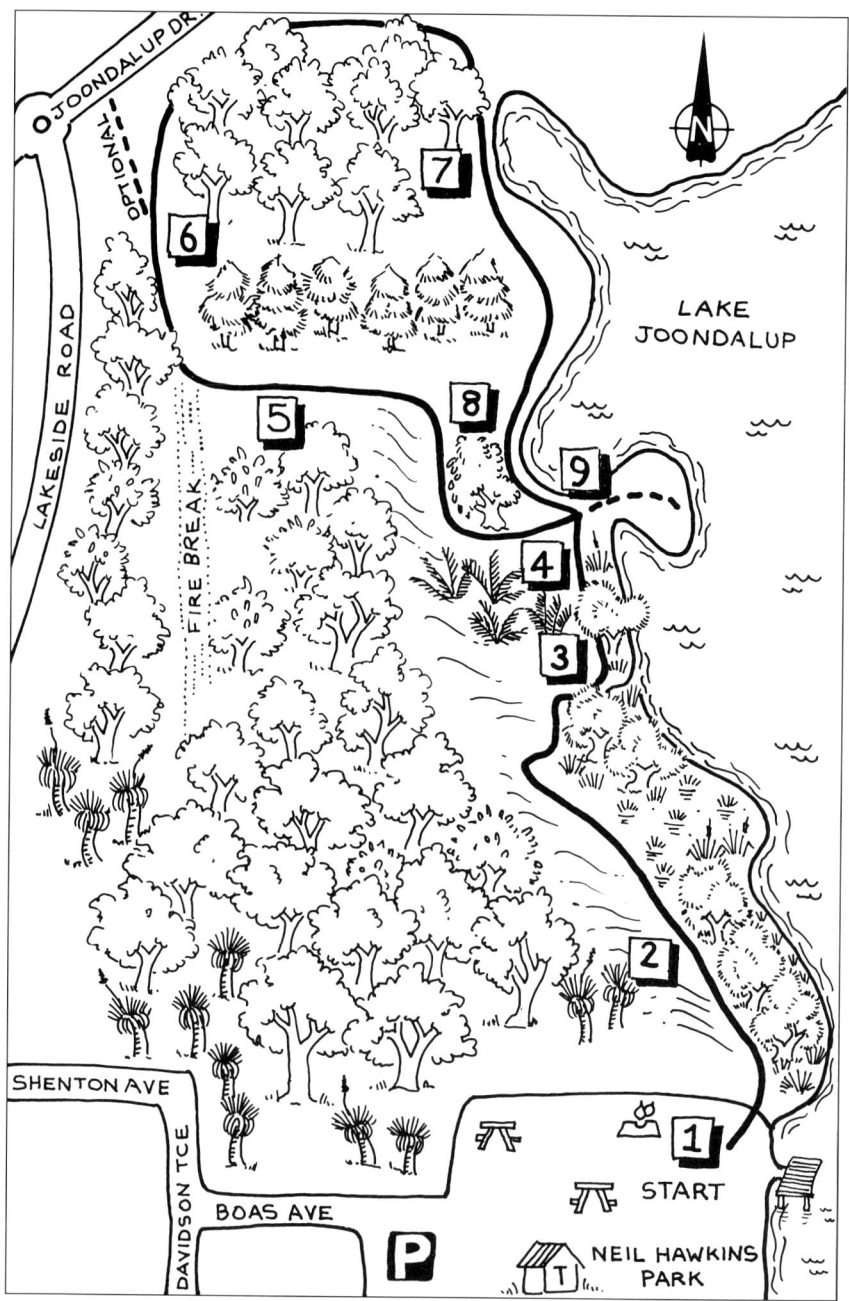

Yaberoo Budjara Heritage Trail

26

Stage 1 – Lake Joondalup, Yellagonga Regional Park

Length: *4 km return.*
Class: *3.*
Walk time: *2 hours.*

This is the first stage of the 28 kilometre Heritage Trail from Lake Joondalup to Wagardu Lake (formerly Loch McNess), in Yanchep National Park. It traverses a mix of wetland and woodland vegetation. Yaberoo Budjara means 'the land of people of the north'. This trail is based on the Aboriginal leader Yellagonga's tribal movements between coastal wetlands.

1   The trail begins at the northern end of Neil Hawkins Park, which was developed as a picnic area in 1979. Prior to European settlement, the wetlands, like many other inland lakes on the coastal plain, played an important role in the lives of Nyoongar people. The name Joondalup was derived from the Aboriginal word for this area, Doondalup. Doondalup means 'lake which glistens'.

2   As you wander along, you may notice two very different vegetation types on opposite sides of the trail. Along the lake's edge on the right are paperbarks, some flooded gums, bulrushes and sedges. On the left side, tuarts and marris grow along the ridge, whereas banksias and dryandras inhabit the flats.

3   Lake Joondalup is a large freshwater lake. It is well-known to Aboriginal people and was used as a favoured camping and hunting ground. The lake provided a rich supply of food such as waterfowl and bulrushes (*Typha* species).

4   The proliferation of zamias here, on the left side of the trail, gives it a prehistoric feel. However, introduced grasses provide evidence of clearing at some time. Just before the trail heads uphill, there are several fine peppermint trees. The paperbarks, flooded gums and sedges continue along the lake's edge, and from them frogs call to their mates during winter.

5   Follow the trail as it continues west. From here, there are good views of the northern parts of the lake. Follow the firebreak towards Joondalup Drive.

6   You may stop at Joondalup Drive or return to Neil Hawkins Park.

7   In spring, the lake is about three metres deep, and the water is replenished by a large aquifer east of Joondalup, called the Gnangara Mound.

8   Lake Joondalup is the breeding ground for some 15 species of waterfowl. Watch and listen for the strange rituals and courtship behaviour of some species. The crested grebe dances on the water, and carries its young on its back, even when diving for food. The musk duck throws water and makes a 'pinging' call.

9 At this point, the trail rejoins the original limestone track and returns to the picnic area.

David and James Gough, Therese Jones

Where is it? *Neil Hawkins Park, Boas Avenue, Joondalup, 25 km north of Perth.*
Travelling time: *40 minutes via the Mitchell Freeway and Joondalup Drive. You can also travel by train to Joondalup and walk through Central Park to Neil Hawkins Park.*
Facilities: *BBQs, picnic tables, playground, toilets, carpark, large grassy area, bird observation platform.*
On-site information: *Trailhead sign, marker arrows along trail.*
Best season: *Autumn, winter, spring.*

BOBTAIL SKINK

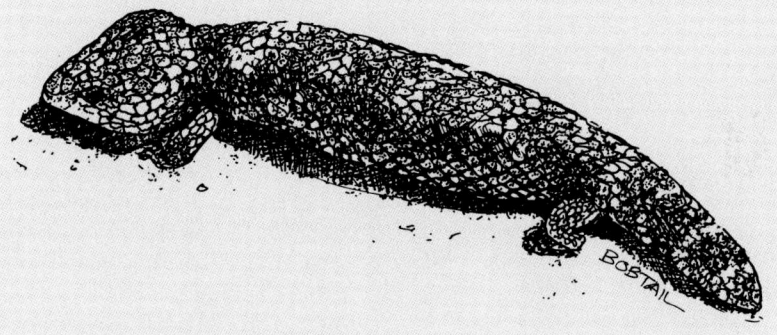

Skinks are one of the largest families of lizards, both in Australia and overseas, and about half of all Australian species are found in WA.

The bobtail skink (*Tiliqua rugosa*) is probably the most commonly seen reptile in the Perth Outdoors area. These stout, scaly, stumpy-tailed skinks are more commonly seen in open habitats like roads and rock outcrops, whereas the slender, shiny-skinned smaller species of skinks prefer leaf litter, or other places with more cover.

The colouration of the bobtail skink is highly variable. The head and back are often orange brown to brown, with creamy spots, blotches or streaks. The belly is white, creamy or grey with blackish flecks, spots or blotches.

If approached, a bobtail will often open its mouth wide and display its blue tongue in an aggressive stance. However, the lizards pose no threat to people.

Unfortunately, these slow-moving creatures are often found dead on the roads.

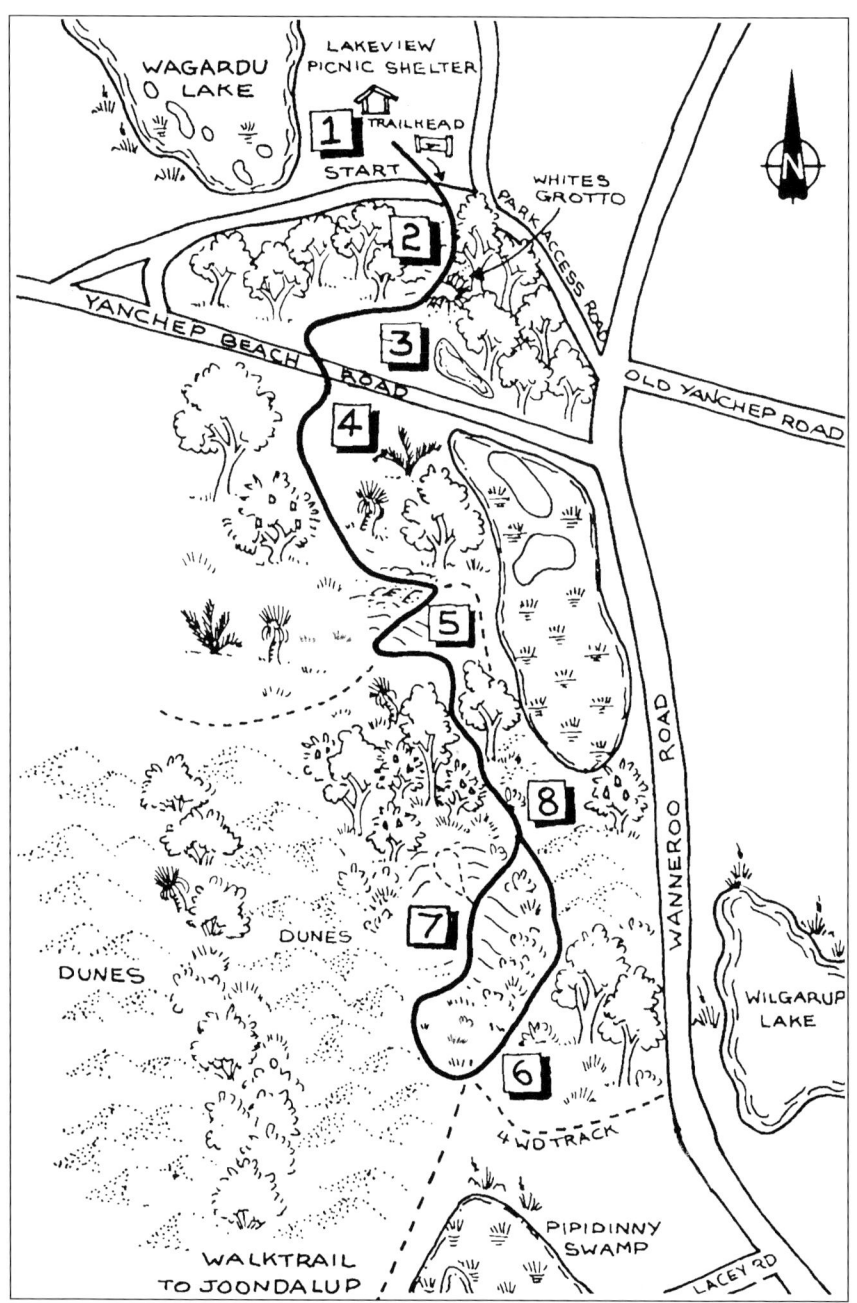

WAGARDU LAKE

LAKEVIEW PICNIC SHELTER

TRAILHEAD

1 START

WHITES GROTTO

2

PARK ACCESS ROAD

YANCHEP BEACH ROAD

3

OLD YANCHEP ROAD

4

5

8

7

6

DUNES

DUNES

WANNEROO ROAD

WILGARUP LAKE

4 WD TRACK

WALKTRAIL TO JOONDALUP

PIPIDINNY SWAMP

LACEY RD

N

100

Yaberoo Budjara Heritage Trail

27

Stage 5 – Wagardu Lake to Pipidinny Wetlands Circuit

Length: *7.5 km circuit from Wagardu Lake.*
Class: *3-4 (some loose sand).*
Walk time: *3 hours, 30 minutes.*

The Yaberoo Budjara Heritage Trail was established in 1988 as a Bicentennial project. The trail consists of five sections extending from Yellagonga Regional Park (Neil Hawkins Park) to Yanchep National Park. This trail is Stage 5 of the heritage trail and takes you through parts of the park which are seldom walked or explored by visitors. It features pockets of tuart forest, banksia woodlands, wetlands and excellent views over the dune system. It is best walked in spring when the dunes are a patchwork of wildflowers. Trail markers are orange with a black balga tree.

Stage 5 of the Yaberoo Budjara Heritage Trail can be walked in two ways. The circuit trail shown here is walked north to south and starts from Wagardu Lake (formerly Loch McNess), near Lakeview picnic shelter. It heads south to Pipidinny wetlands, returning back to the park via the dunes. Alternatively, you can walk south to north, on a one-way trail which starts from Pipidinny Road and heads north through Pipidinny wetlands to the shores of Wagardu Lake. If you would like more information on this 5.5 kilometre route contact CALM's Swan Coastal District Office or purchase a copy of *Discovering Yanchep National Park*.

1   Begin your walk on the trailhead sign near the Lakeview picnic area. Follow the orange markers up the hill to the road. Take great care when crossing. Wagardu Lake has both Aboriginal and European significance. The lake itself is a mythological site and the south-eastern corner was a traditional meeting area for corroborees and rituals. Nyanyi Yandip was the tribal name for this area. It literally means 'pubic hairs' and relates to the reeds surrounding the lake. Yanget is the name given to the bulrush (*Typha orientalis*).

2   Cross the road and follow the trail through a grove of tuarts down a rocky ridge and into a natural hollow called White's Grotto. Many caves and underground streams surround the Grotto. Henry White was the first European to settle in the area, in 1902, and he recorded the grotto and many of the park's caves. Follow the trail along the vehicle track until you reach a large pine tree on the left. Take a left turn at this point.

3   Follow the trail markers to Yanchep Beach Road. Cross the road, taking great care.

4   Follow the markers south along a sandy vehicle track, up a slight ridge until you reach a turn in the trail. At the junction turn right and walk west up the slope.

5   Before the dunes, turn left onto the narrow walktrail. Follow the trail south through picturesque coastal heath and banksia woodlands. Before descending into a grand tuart grove, take a moment to absorb the panoramic view from the top of the ridge.

6   At the four-wheel-drive track turn right and follow the trail west until you get to the dunes.

7   Follow the orange markers up the sandy track toward the top of the dunes. As you near the top, turn right off the sandy track. After a short distance, you can take a short detour to the lookout hill on your left. From this point, you can view the chain of wetlands that begins at Wagardu Lake and continues south, making up Yonderup, Wilgarup and Pipidinny wetlands.

8   Back on the main track, take a left turn at the base of the hill. After a short distance, you'll be back at the top of the loop. Turn left and follow the trail markers, retracing your steps north back to the park.

Therese Jones

Where is it? *At the corner of Pipidinny and Wanneroo Roads, 46 km north of Perth.*
Travelling time: *1 hour from Perth.*
Facilities: *There are toilets, BBQs and picnic shelters in Yanchep National Park. No parking is available at Pipidinny Road.*
On-site information: *Orange trail markers along trail.*
Best season: *Spring.*

WESTERN GREY KANGAROO

WESTERN GREY
KANGAROO

These animals were once common throughout what is now the Perth metropolitan area. They can still be seen in small groups at dusk or dawn in the outer northern, southern and hills areas. A large population can be seen in the late afternoon browsing the fairways of the golf course at Yanchep National Park.

The western grey kangaroo (*Macropus fuliginosus*) is a marsupial. Its young are born in a very incomplete state – minute, blind, hairless and with hind limbs only partially formed. The defenceless young finds its way to the mother's pouch and attaches to a nipple where it develops fully over a period of about 42 weeks.

The male western grey kangaroo can grow to more than two metres from head to tail tip and weigh more than 50 kilograms. It has a strong characteristic odour, hence its nickname 'stinker'.

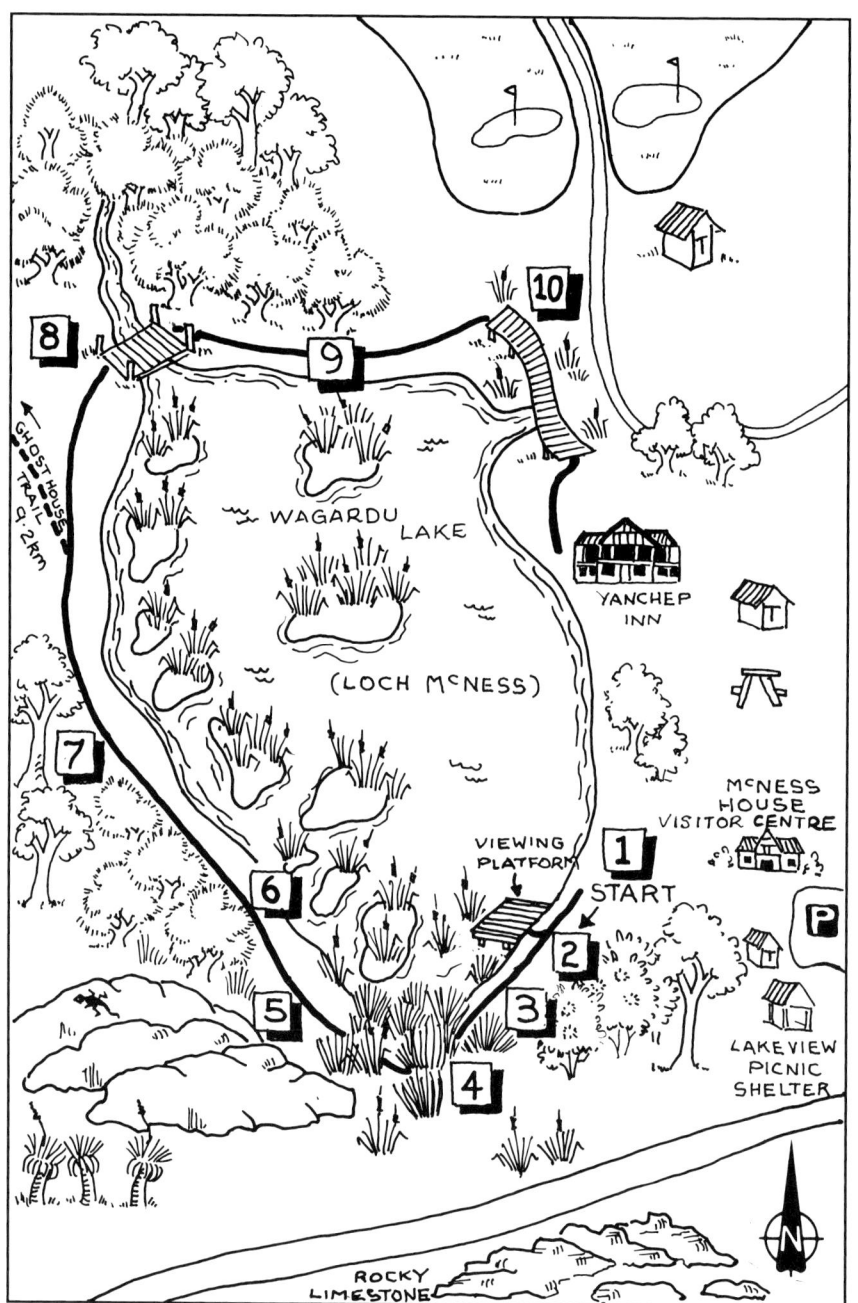

GHOST HOUSE TRAIL 9.2km

8

9

10

WAGARDU LAKE

(LOCH M^cNESS)

YANCHEP INN

M^cNESS HOUSE VISITOR CENTRE

7

6

VIEWING PLATFORM

1

START

2

P

3

5

4

LAKEVIEW PICNIC SHELTER

ROCKY LIMESTONE

N

Wetlands Walktrail

28

Yanchep National Park ($)

Length: *2 km circuit.*
Class: *2.*
Walk time: *1 hour.*

This nature trail takes you through the heart of a living coastal wetland. This walk was formerly known as the Yanjidi Trail. Yanjidi is a variation of yanget, the Nyoongar Aboriginal name for the bulrush (*Typha orientalis*) which is a prominent feature of this walk.

1   Start the trail on the water's edge in Lakeview picnic area (the most southern point of the foreshore).
2   Follow the trail for a short distance, then step off to your right for splendid views of Wagardu Lake (Loch McNess) from the Lakeview viewing platform.
3   Return to the trail and turn right into a thicket of coojong (*Acacia saligna*). This wattle grew prolifically as a result of a hot wildfire in 1991. Coojong is a common coloniser, popping up where the soil has been heated or disturbed. The large ball-like swellings that you may notice on the leaves and stems are caused by a gall rust fungus or a weevil. Some of these shrubs may have died, as they are quick-growing and have a limited lifespan of between seven and ten years.
4   As you approach the lake's edge near the park road, look to your left. A natural stream called Loch Overflow replenishes the lake. The water comes from a large underground aquifer in the Gnangara Mound. The natural movement of water through the limestone strata has also contributed to the development of caves within the park.
5   As you walk on, you will pass through a small grove of flooded gum (*Eucalyptus rudis*). The Aboriginal name for this tree is 'moitch'.
6   Heading up the western side of the lake, you will pass beneath some overhanging paperbarks (*Melaleuca rhaphiophylla*), which provide a safe haven for many wetland birds such as coots and western swamphens, which nestle into the hollows of the trunk to avoid predators and strong winds.
7   As the trail begins to climb up a rocky limestone ridge, you may notice the scars that the 1991 wildfire left on the mature tuart trees.
8   During the park's development in the 1930s, the lake was dredged of excess rushes to allow recreation activities to occur on the lake. The remains of the dredger now form part of the bridge that crosses the lake at this narrow point.
9   As you continue along the trail, you will come to an opening with fields of yanget.

Aboriginal people pounded the roots of this bulrush to form a starchy paste used to make a form of dough to eat.

10 Follow the trail to the boardwalk. Before you come to the end of the trail, stop, look and listen! You will be delighted by the sights and sounds that abound in this wetland. If you are lucky, you may hear the unique call of the musk duck or spot an inquisitive long-necked tortoise coming up for air.

Therese Jones

Where is it? *Yanchep National Park, 51 km north of Perth on Wanneroo Road.*
Travelling time: *1 hour from Perth.*
Facilities: *Picnic area, toilets and carpark in park.*
On-site information: *Trailhead sign, green yanget trail markers along route.*
Best season: *Spring, summer, autumn.*

PACIFIC BLACK DUCK

Every Australian would be familiar with the Pacific black duck (*Anas superciliosa*), which inhabits wetlands throughout most of the continent, including those in almost every city suburb. In most city areas they are very tame and approach people to be fed. Their natural diet consists largely of seeds, aquatic insects and crustaceans.

The top of the head and the back of the neck are dark brown. A dark brown stripe from the bill to the eye, on a cream background, and a thinner paler stripe beneath give this bird its typical striped face with its lovely benign expression. The brown feathers that cover most of the body have cream edges and there is a broad green/purple patch on each wing.

Pacific black ducks are common and widespread. They are also fairly nomadic, especially in more marginal areas. In some areas, interbreeding with the introduced mallard (*Anas platyrhynchos*) presents a problem to this species.

Black ducks live in a wide range of habitats including streams, swamps, rivers, lakes, even drainage ditches, with fresh, brackish and sometimes even salt water. They do, however, prefer deep freshwater swamps.

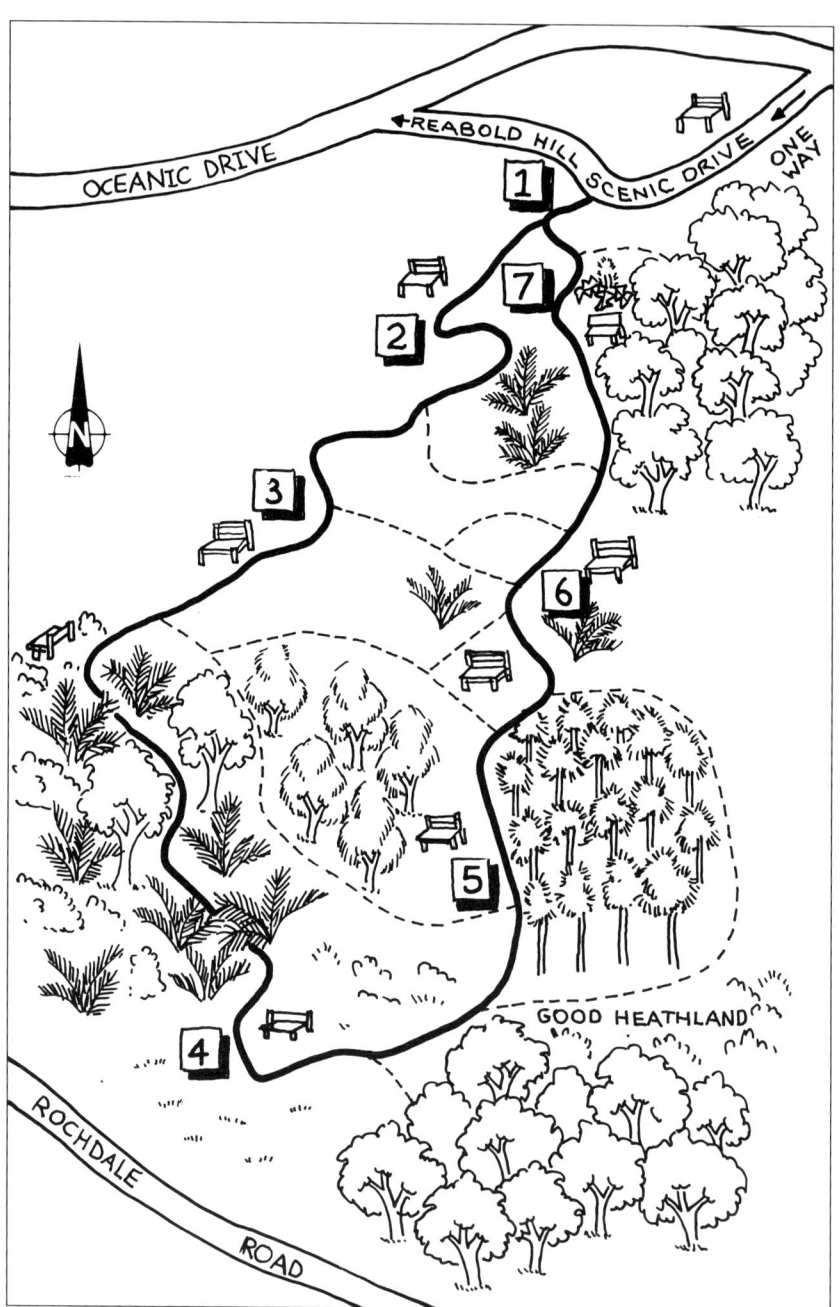

Zamia Trail

29

Bold Park

Length: 5 km loop.
Class: 3.
Walk time: 2 hours.

This walk begins at Reabold Hill and provides views to the ocean and inland as well as changes in vegetation types and abundant bird life.

1. Start at the lookout on Reabold Hill, the highest point on the Swan Coastal Plain (93 metres above sea level). It offers panoramic views to Rottnest Island, Garden Island, the Darling Range, Perry Lakes and Perth City. The trail heads downhill from the carpark.
2. A short way down the track on the right is a view trail to the first of several seats. From here, there are good views to Rottnest Island. Vegetation along the trail includes banksias and acacias, which are popular with honeyeaters.
3. At the corner of Thornbill Walk, a lookout provides views over surrounding bushland of scattered tuarts with banksia understorey, and beyond to Cottesloe and to Garden Island. This section features an abundance of zamias. You may spot kangaroo paws and orchids on your way to the next point of interest.
4. This site is an old turf farm and consists of an open grassy area. Further on and to the south are stands of limestone marlock (*Eucalyptus decipiens*).
5. At the intersection with the Sheoak Walk, take time to listen to the sounds of the bush. The pine plantation to the right of the trail was planted in the early 1900s, to provide shade for ladies as they 'took' tea. You will see sheoaks to your left.
6. Another view trail to the left of the track takes you to a seat facing north and giving views over bushland. There are more zamias to the left of the trail, and Fremantle mallees (*Eucalyptus foecunda*) to the right.
7. Here, the Zamia Trail meets Camel Lake Trail. There is a seat beneath a banksia tree.

Peter Sharp, Jody Mansell-Fletcher

Where is it? 10 km from Perth off Oceanic Drive.
Travelling time: 15 minutes from Perth.
Facilities: Carpark.
On-site information: Sign at trailhead, directional signs along trail.
Best season: All year, spring for wildflowers.

109

NUMBATS

NUMBAT

The numbat (*Myrmecobius fasciatus*) is a small termite-eating marsupial that was once widespread throughout the open wandoo forest of the western Wheatbelt.

The banded anteater, as it is sometimes called, dines largely on termites and, before extensive clearing for agriculture and the introduction of the cat and the fox, was once widespread from Albany to Watheroo and east beyond Kalgoorlie to western New South Wales.

The numbat is a gentle and curious animal weighing up to half a kilogram and measuring about 20 centimetres in body length. Its fur is greyish and reddish-brown, with white flecks. Across the back and rump are stripes of black and white. Its head is small and pointed, with white stripes above and below the eye and a black stripe through the eye.

Food is obtained by turning over sticks and branches on the ground, then rapidly licking up the exposed termites. Where termite galleries are close to the surface, the ground is dug up.

Two populations of numbats can be seen during the day in the Dryandra State Forest near Narrogin and the Perup jarrah forest, east of Manjimup. In these areas where fox numbers are controlled, numbats and other smaller mammals are becoming increasingly common.

The River   Walks 30 – 36

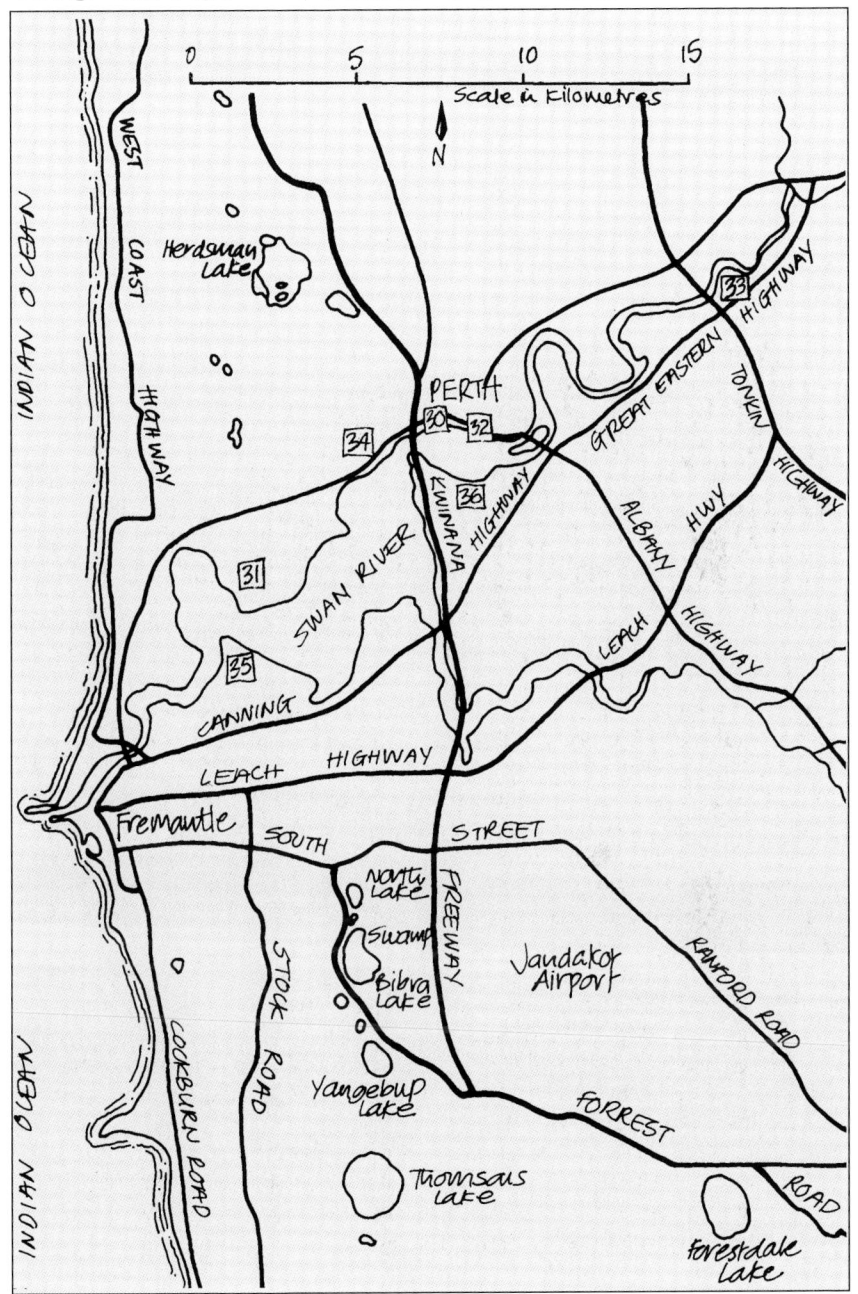

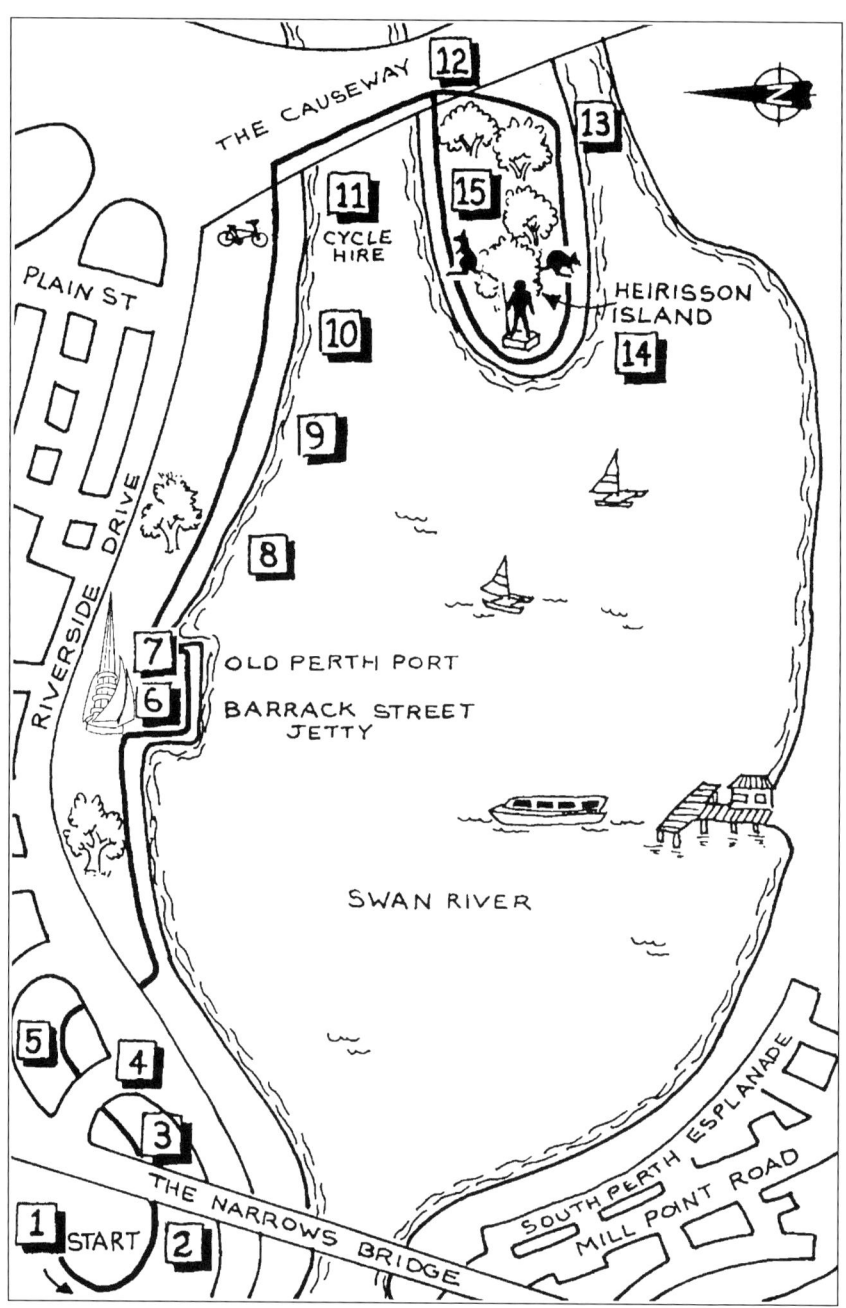

THE CAUSEWAY

12

13

PLAIN ST

11
CYCLE
HIRE

15

HEIRISSON
ISLAND

10

14

RIVERSIDE DRIVE

9

8

7

OLD PERTH PORT

6

BARRACK STREET
JETTY

SWAN RIVER

5

4

3

SOUTH PERTH ESPLANADE

MILL POINT ROAD

1 START

2

THE NARROWS BRIDGE

Between the Bridges Walk 30

Perth Water

Length: *10 km return.*
Class: *3.*
Walk time: *3 hours.*

This walk links the two major river crossings at each end of the city. It runs mostly along the water's edge. Except for Heirisson Island, the walk is along a dual-use cycle/walktrack and is suitable for wheelchairs, prams and strollers. It is best walked on a Sunday when there should be less traffic noise.

1   The walk begins at the small carpark by the ornamental lake and Narrows interchange in Mounts Bay Road. The Four Seasons Trail passes through here.
2   Walk south and pass under the Narrows Bridge, taking in views down the river to the redeveloped Swan Brewery and across to the South Perth foreshore.
3   A small wetland within the Narrows interchange has the city skyline as a backdrop and is teeming with bird life including black swans.
4   You soon reach the first of three underpasses. Facilities here include a toilet block, drinking fountain and bench seating.
5   There is a small open space between three underpasses: one leading to the city, the second to the foreshore and the third back towards the brewery. A large obelisk gives details about the construction of the freeway interchange and the river's geomorphology. Take the underpass to the river and follow the path along the river's edge. Looking towards the city, you can see the Perth Convention Centre, which was officially opened in 2004.
6   The Four Seasons Trailhead sign is just before Barrack Street Jetty. The trail, also in this book, runs to Kennedy Fountain. Barrack Square serves as a departure point for river cruises, and ferries to South Perth and Rottnest Island.
7   Have a short break and perhaps a snack at the Old Perth Port with its shops, restaurants and toilets. The Swan Bell Tower, which was first opened to the public on 10 December 2000, is open every day between 10 am and 4.30 pm. It was built to house the 12 Bells of St Martins from London's Trafalgar Square. Recorded as being in existence from before the 14th century, they have rung out to celebrate England's victory over the Spanish Armada in 1588, the homecoming of Captain James Cook after his voyage of discovery in 1771 and the World War II victory at El Alamein. The bell tower offers visitors fascinating displays on the history of the bells and bell ringing, as well as great views of Perth city and the Swan River.

8   The WA Rowing Club, classified by the National Trust, is an interesting old wooden building that was built around 1905. Between it and Victoria Avenue there is a landscaped area featuring date palms and sculptured seating.

9   Langley Park was Perth's first aerodrome. From time to time the park is used to commemorate historic aviation events, which see dozens of vintage aircraft on display or flying. Other exhibitions and sporting events are also held here.

10 As you come to the junction of Plain Street and Riverside Drive, Heirisson Island can be seen across the river. The trail diverges from Riverside Drive and passes through the Point Fraser demonstration wetland. Woven through the site are historical and indigenous points of interest that include stories and quotes highlighting events that have occurred here, along with explanations on how the wetland helps to filter nutrients from the water before it enters the river. Numerous interesting birds make use of the wetland, including great egrets and dotterels.

11 Next to the carpark there are cycle hire facilities, a children's playground and a drinking fountain. Walk onto the Causeway Bridge and head south.

12 Access to Heirisson Island is on the right. The compacted limestone pathways on the island are unsuitable for wheelchairs.

13 Walk to the south bank of the island, and enter the fence through a gate. The fence was erected to keep in the kangaroos which were introduced to the island. However, the best time to see the kangaroos is in the evening or early morning, when these largely nocturnal animals emerge to graze. This part of the island is a grassed open space with several internal wetlands and extensive clumps of trees. Waterbirds such as ducks, egrets and cormorants are highly visible. Head around the western portion of the island in a clockwise direction.

14 The western end of the island gives superb views of Perth Water, with the city and Kings Park providing a picturesque backdrop. On a broad grassy knoll is a large bronze statue of the Aboriginal warrior Yagan, whose people once camped in areas by the Swan and Canning rivers.

15 The northern bank of the island is more open and exposed to the wind. Leave the enclosure and continue to the Causeway Bridge, retracing your steps to the carpark on Mounts Bay Road along the river foreshore. Walking in a westerly direction gives a different perspective, with Kings Park becoming a more dominant feature.

Wayne Schmidt and family, Carolyn Thomson-Dans, Lauren Dunn

Where is it? *The starting point is 1 km from Perth City centre, just off Mounts Bay Road on the north of the Narrows.*
Travelling time: *5 minutes from Perth CBD.*
Facilities: *Seating, water and children's play areas at various points along the walk. There are toilets within the Narrows interchange and at Old Perth Port.*
Best season: *All year (Sundays for less traffic noise).*

CORMORANTS

One of the attractions of the Swan and Canning rivers is the sight of cormorants perched on posts, boats and shoreline obstacles, often in heraldic poses, as they dry in the sun with wings outstretched.

The little pied cormorant (*Phalacrocorax melanoleucos*) is the most common of the four species that inhabit our waterways on the west coast. This medium-sized bird is about 60 centimetres long, and has a black back, white underparts and a yellowish beak.

Similar in size and habits, and almost as common, is the little black cormorant (*P. sulcirostris*), which is completely black. Little black cormorants are sometimes seen in flocks of 1000 or more, as they fish on the Swan River.

The two largest species are both about 80 centimetres long. They are the pied cormorant (*P. varius*), which looks similar to the little pied cormorant except it has a yellowish-orange patch in front of the eye, and the black cormorant (*P. carbo*), which is the biggest of all the species.

Cormorants feed by diving, usually from the surface, and swimming underwater for periods up to half a minute or more. They are propelled by large webbed feet. At the surface they swim with alternating leg strokes, while underwater they use both feet together. Depending on where they feed, they prey on small fish, crustaceans, amphibians and insects.

As well as frequenting the Swan and Canning rivers, cormorants are also found on Perth's lakes and swamps.

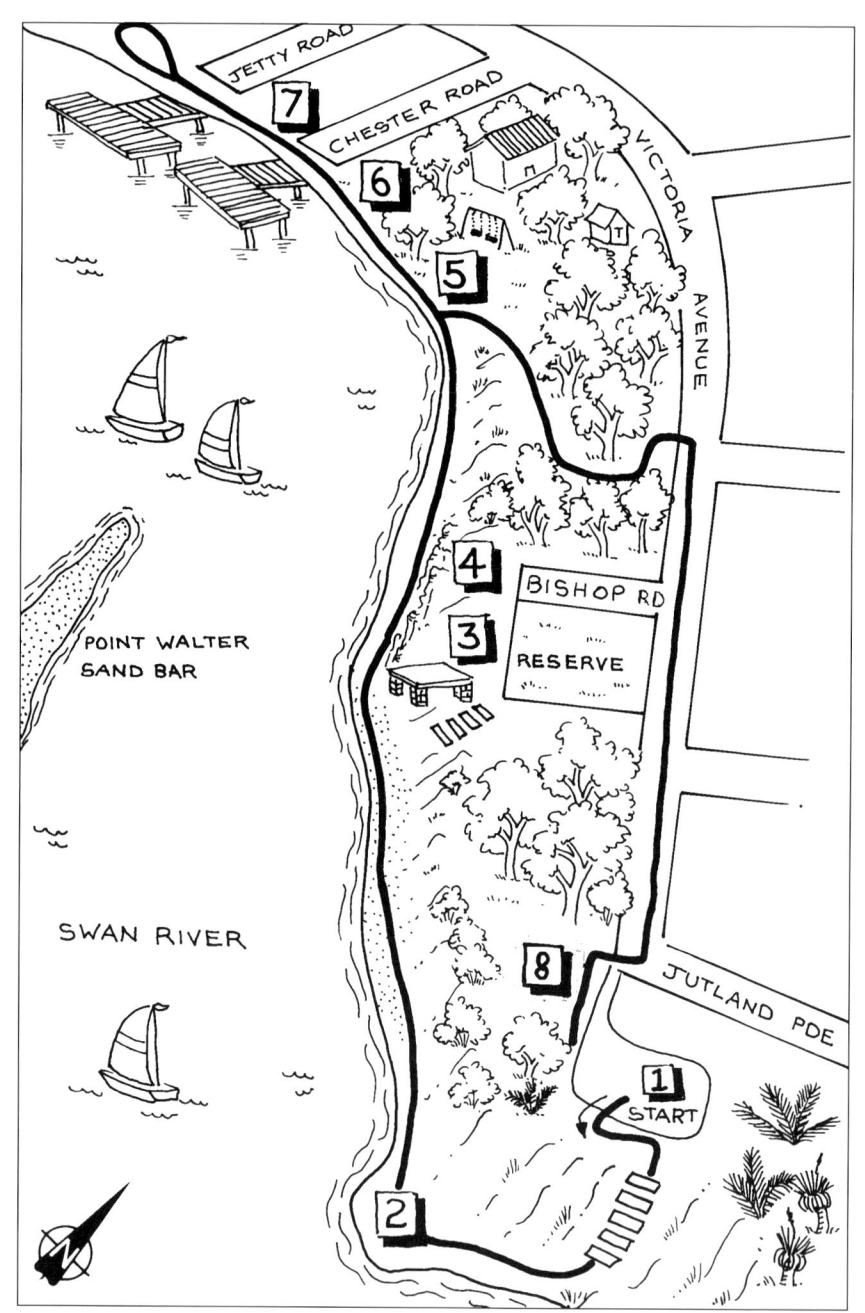

JETTY ROAD

7

CHESTER ROAD

6

5

VICTORIA AVENUE

4

3

BISHOP RD

RESERVE

POINT WALTER
SAND BAR

SWAN RIVER

8

JUTLAND PDE

1
START

2

N

Claremont Foreshore Trail

Length: *5 km loop.*
Class: *3.*
Walk time: *1 hour, 30 minutes.*

This walk offers a riverside experience with views across to Alfred Cove, Lucky Bay, Point Walter, Mosman Bay and Freshwater Bay. Parts of the walk offer a sense of what the river would have looked like to Captain Stirling as he sailed upstream from Fremantle in 1827.

1 There are panoramic views of the river from the small carpark adjacent to Point Resolution Reserve. A metal plaque indicates the point was named after the ship *Resolution* and was also the location of a convict depot. A limestone and concrete pathway runs down from the carpark to the river foreshore.

2 Downstream, the beach is mainly sandy, sometimes rocky and rarely wider than three or four metres. There are several other paths leading up to the reserve.

3 The low lookout (brick pillars supporting a concrete roof) marks Bishop Road Reserve. A bitumen path leads up to the reserve.

4 About 100 metres further along the foreshore, the beach narrows to about one metre past tall limestone 'pinnacles'. Be sure to check the tide before continuing. The beach here is narrow, often rocky and frequently covered with reeds and grass. River views are excellent, but you need to stand still to enjoy them in case you stumble.

5 The foreshore widens to a grassed reserve (Mrs Herbert's Park) with a playground, trees and toilets halfway up the hill. Claremont Museum is at the top of the hill. The Mews boatshed, on the Museum site, is near the water's edge.

6 A foreshore reserve leads along to a small carpark at the bottom of Chester Road. A plaque on stone marks the site of the old Claremont Baths.

7 Claremont Jetty, on Jetty Road adjacent to Claremont Yacht Club. There are views to Keanes Point and the Royal Freshwater Bay Yacht Club and downstream to Blackwall Reach. From here, retrace your steps to Mrs Herbert's Park and visit the Museum. Information on other local walktrails is available from the Museum. Walk back along Victoria Avenue to Point Resolution.

8 Point Resolution Reserve contains a mix of native and eastern States trees and shrubs. At the northern end of the reserve, a clump of trees shades a brick paved circle with a picnic table.

Ann Nicholson, Clare-Francis Sunndells

Where is it? *9 km south-west of Perth on the northern bank of the Swan River.*
Travelling time: *20 minutes from Perth.*
Facilities: *Picnic area, tables, water, carpark, BBQs, toilets at Mrs Herberts Park.*
Best season: *All year – check tide times.*

BLACK SWAN

The black swan (*Cygnus atratus*) was first recorded by the Dutch navigator Vlamingh in January 1697 in the Swan Estuary. Although it is found throughout Australia, this graceful bird is regarded with special affection by many generations of Western Australians. It is the State's bird emblem and has long been used to identify things Western Australian.

Black swans can be seen on most waterways throughout the lower half of the State. They frequent open areas of fresh, brackish and salt water such as flooded paddocks, green crops and tidal mudflats, but prefer permanent lakes and swamps with emergent and subaquatic vegetation.

Males and females are similar in size and appearance, but males can be identified in flight by their longer necks, and hold their necks more erect when swimming. Black swans make a musical honk or bugling sound, which can often be heard at night.

Nests are a bulky collection of sticks and rushes, built in fresh or brackish swamps and lakes. Between four and nine eggs are laid in late winter. The eggs are pale green, becoming paler through the incubation period. Incubation takes about 40 days, after which the downy grey cygnets hatch.

Each year, between September and February, black swans moult, becoming flightless. During this time, they often gather on open waterways in their thousands.

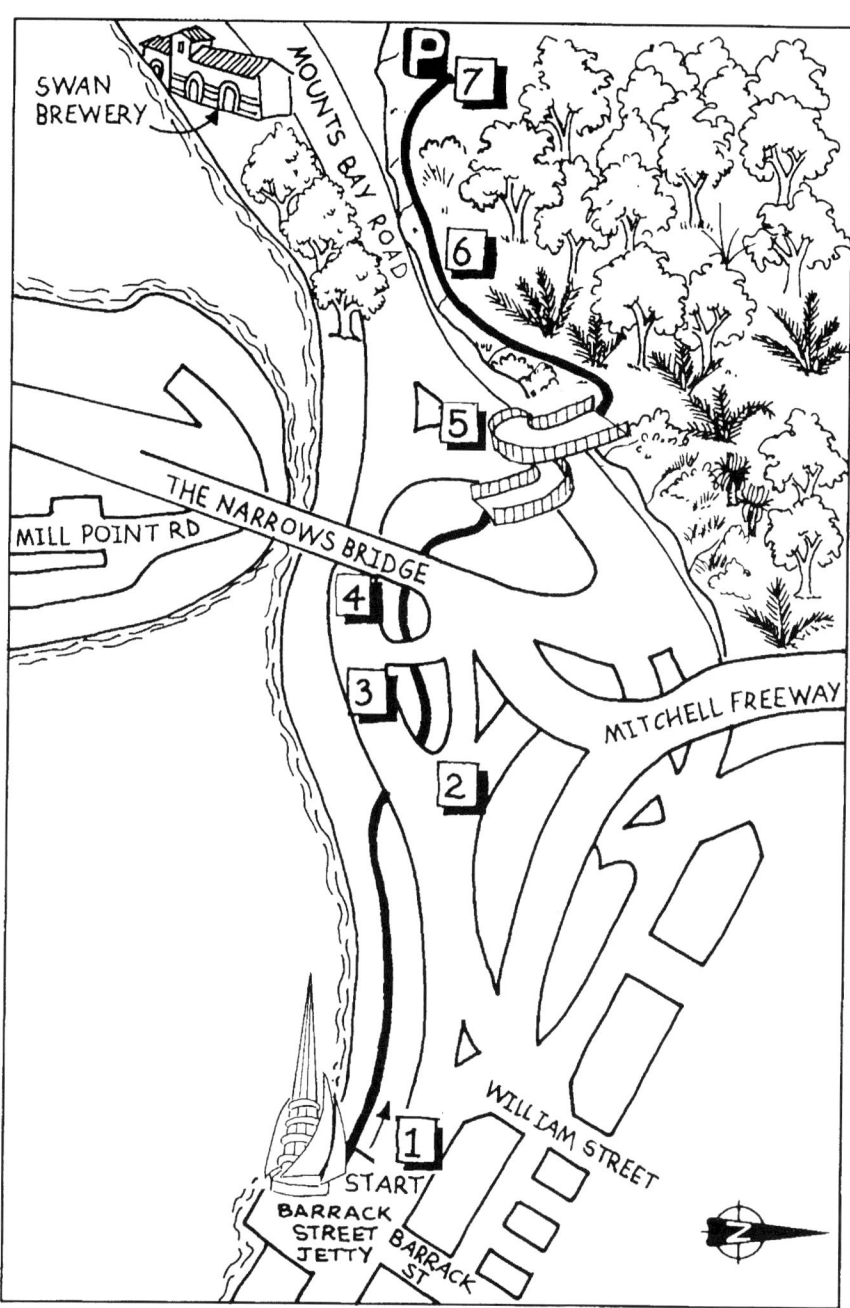

SWAN BREWERY

MOUNTS BAY ROAD

P

7

6

5

THE NARROWS BRIDGE

MILL POINT RD

4

3

2

MITCHELL FREEWAY

WILLIAM STREET

1

START

BARRACK STREET JETTY

BARRACK ST

N

Four Seasons Trail

Length: *5.2 km return.*
Class: *2.*
Walk time: *2 hours (with stops at information stations).*

This trail features information stations which are changed according to the season (hence the name), benches and good views of the river. It begins at Barrack Street Jetty and finishes at Kennedy Fountain near the old Swan Brewery.

1   Head west from the Barrack Street Jetty along Riverside Drive. There are good views across the river to South Perth and along to the Narrows Bridge. Kings Park can be seen rising above the riverside beyond the Narrows.
2   Turn right into the first underpass, then take the first left and walk through the Narrows interchange.
3   Walk past lakes then through the next underpass.
4   Turn left and walk under the Narrows Bridge towards the footbridge.
5   Cross the footbridge over Mounts Bay Road, viewing the escarpment of Kings Park. Turn left after crossing the bridge.
6   Follow the path below the escarpment south-west along Mounts Bay Road. Here you can see a variety of vegetation types.
7   The Kennedy Fountain is adjacent to a small picnic area opposite the redeveloped Swan Brewery. The fountain was Perth's first public water supply and was erected in 1861 by Governor A E Kennedy. From here, you may choose to return along the same route or cross Mounts Bay Road (taking care to avoid busy traffic) and follow the footpath along the river's edge to Barrack Street Jetty.

Tracy Churchill, Russell Kingdom

Where is it? *In Perth City on the northern shore of Perth Water.*
Travelling time: *5 minutes from Perth GPO.*
Facilities: *Parking and toilets at Barrack Street Jetty, BBQs and parking at Kennedy Fountain.*
On-site information: *Trailhead sign and 'Four Seasons' interpretive panels along route.*
Best season: *All year.*

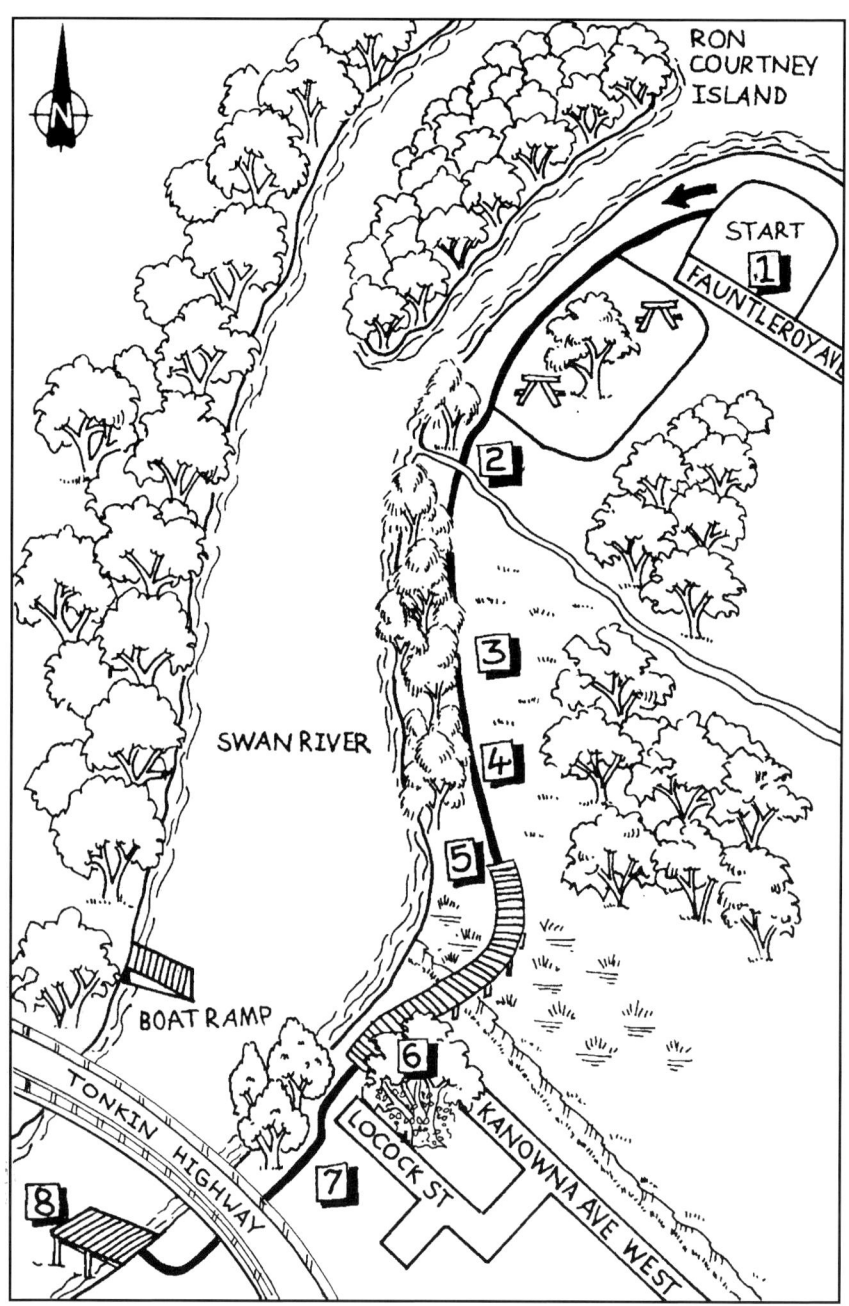

RON COURTNEY ISLAND

START

1

FAUNTLEROY AVE

2

3

4

5

SWAN RIVER

BOAT RAMP

6

LOCOCK ST

KANOWNA AVE WEST

7

TONKIN HIGHWAY

8

N

Garvey Park Riverside Walk

33

Length: 2.5 km return.
Class: 2 (accessible to wheelchairs).
Walk time: 1 hour.

This pleasant riverside walk passes through grassland, sheoak woodland and samphire swampland. Bird life is abundant in the woodlands, and there are many varieties of waterbirds along the river banks and in the swamp area. The pathway has a bitumen surface and is ideal for wheelchairs, prams and strollers.

1   Proceed downstream from Garvey Park, with its playground and shaded picnic area set among flooded gums and overlooking Ron Courtney Island.
2   As you cross a creek the path winds into a small grove of sheoaks. Here, there are magpies, willy wagtails, galahs, little corellas and a variety of waterbirds.
3   Along this stretch, the river's edge is lined with sheoaks, reeds and sedges. On the eastern side of the track there is an open grassland with flooded gums beyond.
4   The path turns away from the river's edge and winds through the edge of a dense sheoak woodland. Here, there is an abundance of birds including white-faced herons and 'twenty-eight' parrots.
5   As the vegetation changes to samphire swamp, a boardwalk elevates the pathway over the water. This area is home to many waterbirds, including egrets, grebes and herons. Snakes are likely in warmer months.
6   At the end of the boardwalk is a very large flooded gum with creepers climbing in the lower branches. From here there are excellent views upstream and across the river to Claughton Reserve. If you look under the road bridge you can see the tall buildings of Perth's city skyline.
7   Just before the bridge there is a small grove of olive trees.
8   Walking under the bridge you will come to a small jetty, from where you can observe passing boats or waterbirds. Retrace your steps to Garvey Park.

John and Joel Hunter

Where is it? 11 km east of Perth on Fauntleroy Avenue.
Travelling time: 20 minutes via Great Eastern Highway.
Facilities: Wood BBQs, tables, playground, carpark, toilets, shop/cafe.
Best season: Spring for birds and flowers, summer, autumn.

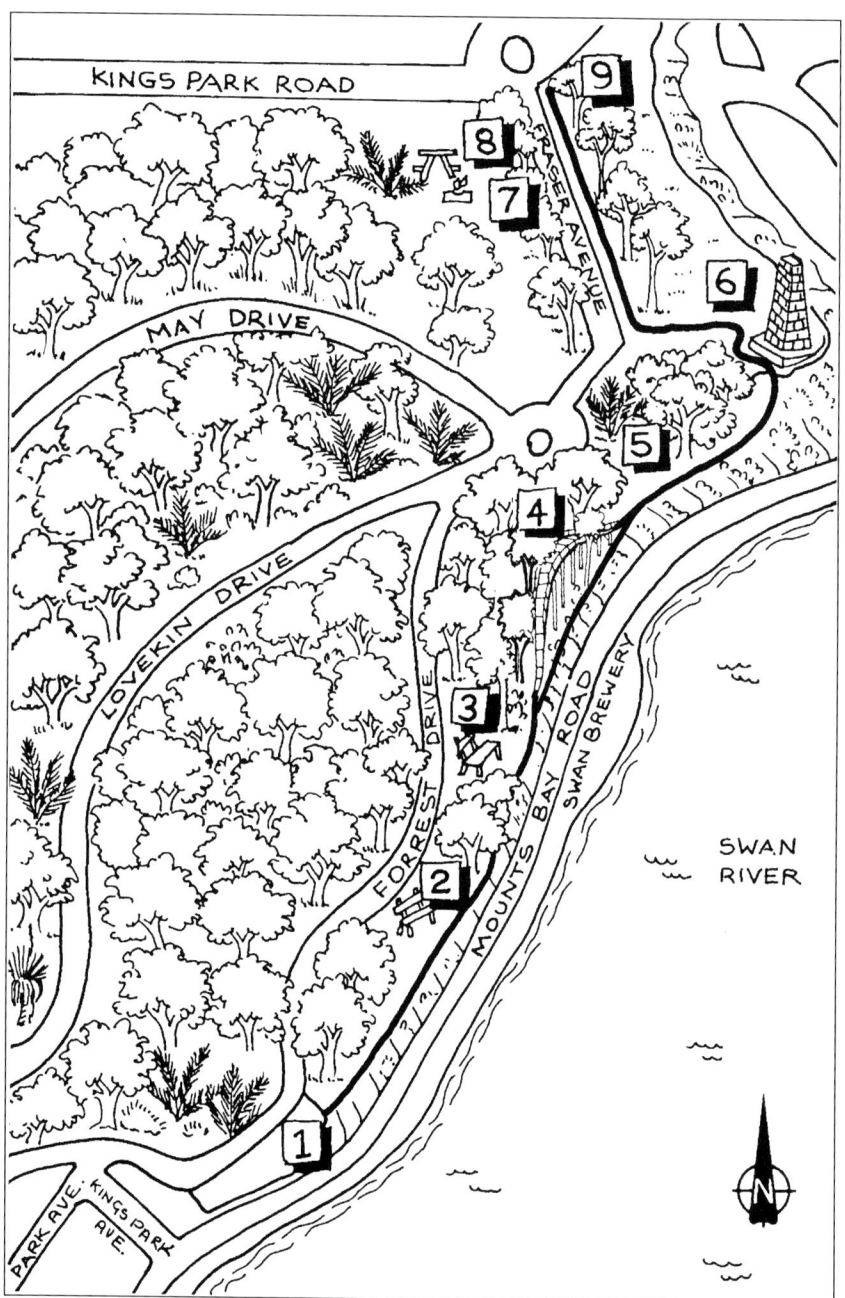

KINGS PARK ROAD

MAY DRIVE

LOVEKIN DRIVE

FRASER AVENUE

FORREST DRIVE

MOUNTS BAY ROAD

SWAN BREWERY

SWAN RIVER

PARK AVE. KINGS PARK AVE.

N

Kings Park Scarp Track

Length: *3.6 km return.*
Class: *3.*
Walk time: *1 hour, 45 minutes.*

There are many walktrails through Kings Park, but this one offers views of the river as well as passing through native bush and landscaped areas of the park. The first part of the walk is quiet, with fewer people, whereas you will encounter tourists and other sightseers after passing the War Memorial.

1   Just below the lower carpark on Forrest Drive is a lookout with a metal, leaf-shaped awning, from which you can gain expansive views of the Swan River, the yachts in Matilda Bay and the city skyline. Head east along the track set high above Mounts Bay Road. Vegetation along this section includes sheoaks, kangaroo paws, banksias and dryandras.

2   A number of seats along the path are well-placed to overlook the Narrows Bridge, South Perth, Perth Water, the city skyline and, in the distance, the Darling Scarp.

3   Divert off the Law Trail to head up to and via the Lotterywest Federation Walkway, which is open every day between 9 am and 5 pm. From the walkway there are great views of the river and fascinating information is provided about surrounding native plants, such as marris and grasstrees. The Old Swan Brewery, now redeveloped, can be seen below through the trees.

4   Back on the Law Trail, a rotunda is the next point of interest. There are more panoramic views from the city in the east to the suburbs of Applecross and Attadale in the west.

5   Here, there is a beautiful view down the scarp. At the first fork in the bitumen path an optional path leads down to the Kennedy Fountain and adjacent picnic site, but remember you will have to walk back up the scarp!

6   The State War Memorial is set high above the Narrows, overlooking Perth and surrounding waters. There are manicured gardens and a number of other memorials and dedicated trees.

7   Near the Queen Victoria Memorial, walkers will notice a stark contrast between this and the first part of the walk. This section features manicured gardens and an avenue of lemon-scented gums, planted in 1938.

8   The 10th Light Horse Memorial. Close by is a picnic area with barbecues.

9   This is the main gateway to Kings Park. There is an information shelter on the

city side of Fraser Avenue. Look back from here for impressive views of the lemon-scented gums. Retrace your steps to the start.

James Harrower, Pauline Kozadinos, Jacqueline Pontré, Lauren Dunn

Where is it? *4 km from the city centre on Forrest Drive.*
Travelling time: *15 minutes via Mounts Bay Road, Kings Park Avenue and Park Road.*
Facilities: *BBQs, restaurant, kiosk, toilets, carparks at various places in the park.*
On-site information: *Information booth on Fraser Avenue.*
Best season: *All year, spring for wildflowers.*

'TWENTY-EIGHT' PARROT

The 'twenty-eight' parrot is a subspecies of the Port Lincoln parrot. The normal call of the Port Lincoln is a whistling *kwink-kwing*. However, many birds around Perth emit a trisyllabic call with a rising inflection at the end that resembles the words 'twenty-eight', hence the name. Other differences include a pronounced red frontal band above the beak, a larger size and a heavier bill.

'Twenty-eight' parrots eat fruit, nuts, berries, nectar, blossoms, buds, insects and insect larvae. They have a strong liking for seeds, especially those of marri (*Corymbia calophylla*).

At the start of the breeding season, pairs of parrots inspect hollows in living or dead trees. When a nest site has been chosen, the pair defend it vigorously while the hollow is prepared for nesting. Between four and seven (usually five) eggs are laid and incubation takes about 19 days.

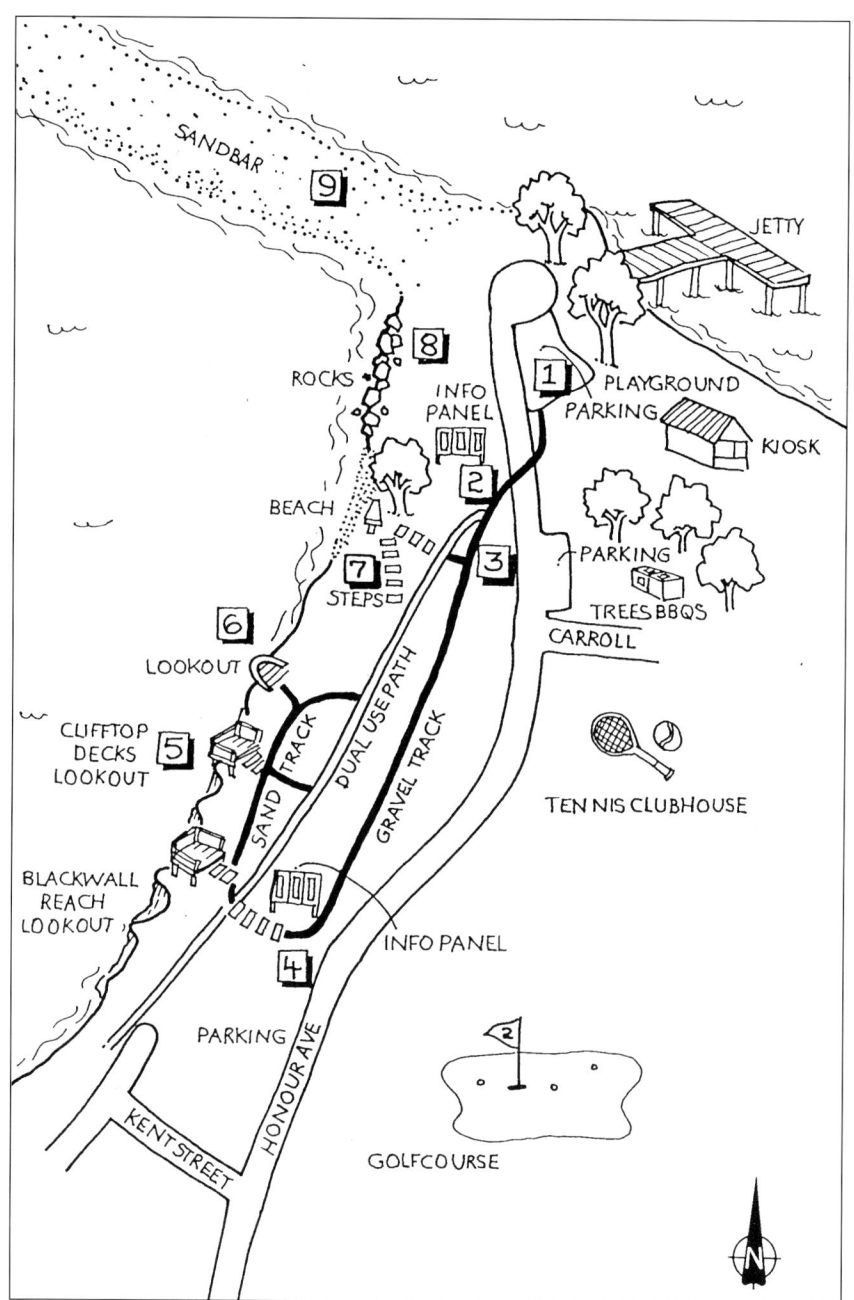

Point Walter to Blackwall Reach

Length: *2 km loop (plus a 1 km return walk along the sandbar).*
Class: *3.*
Walk time: *1 hour, 30 minutes.*

This wonderful walk is close to excellent family facilities at Point Walter. It provides scenic vistas over the Swan River, a glimpse into the original riverside vegetation and the bird life is prolific. It is enjoyed by young and old alike and can accommodate prams and strollers.

1   Park in the upper section of the carpark near the kiosk, and walk a short distance uphill along Honour Avenue. Take great care to avoid traffic, as there is no path until you reach the start of a dual-use cycle/walk track on your right.

2   Take some time to peruse the information shelter provided by the City of Melville at the beginning of the path, as this area has some fascinating history. Take the gravel track above and roughly parallel to the concrete dual use path. The first section of the walk is through bushland of peppermint (*Agonis flexuosa*), tuart (*Eucalyptus gomphocephala*), jarrah (*Eucalyptus marginata*), parrotbush (*Dryandra sessilis*), harsh hakea (*Hakea prostrata*), zamia palms (*Macrozamia reidlei*), wattles and banksias (*Banksia attenuata, B. menziesii* and *B. grandis*). Wildflowers include native wisteria (*Hardenbergia comptoniana*), mouse-ears (*Calothamnus rupestris*) and the yellowish-orange pea flowers of green stinkwood (*Jacksonia sternbergiana*). CALM's Bush Books, *Common Trees of the South-West Forests*, *Common Wildflowers of the South-West Forests* and *Bush Tucker Plants of the South-West* will help you identify some of the flora species. Unfortunately, many weeds have also invaded this area and compete vigorously with the native vegetation. Keep your eyes open for birds such as magpies, wattlebirds and other honeyeaters, and Port Lincoln parrots.

3   A little way along, you will reach a five-way intersection of tracks and a sign about the trams that once serviced Point Walter. Continue along the old tramway path that still runs parallel to, and above, the dual use path.

4   When you reach the carpark and another information sign at the end of this track, turn right, towards the river, and continue down the steps to the Blackwall Reach Lookout over the Swan River and the scenic limestone cliffs along its edge (if you have a stroller or pram there is an alternative but less direct track without steps).

You can see across to Chidley Point, Mosman Bay and Freshwater Bay. You may also see the striking red flowers of cockies tongues (*Templetonia retusa*). The limestone pinnacle in front of the platform is known as the 'White Lady'. Information panels explain that the locality was used to load blue metal onto ferries during World War II.

5   Start the walk back along the dual-use path, then take a sandy track that forks to the left. This will take you to Cliff Top Decks Lookout, where you can see right into the caves along the water's edge. If you are lucky you may also see bottlenose dolphins frolicking in the river.

6   A third cliff top platform provided by the City of Melville is also accessed by the sandy track. It incorporates a gate and a short ladder down to the rocky shoreline. If you opt to explore please take great care and supervise children closely. Do not enter the cave, which is a risk area.

7   Continue back along the dual use path. When you are directly below point 3 a set of steps takes you down to an attractive and secluded beach on the river's edge. A grassy area under the nearby trees and a bench seat makes this an ideal spot to linger.

8   From here, follow the dual use path back to the information sign. Or you can opt to continue along the narrow rocky beach back to Point Walter.

9   This part of the walk is optional. It traverses the sandbar and gives excellent views upstream and downstream. Migratory waders, such as sandpipers, stints, plovers and godwits, can sometimes be seen on or around the sandbar.

Allan Wicks, Carolyn Thomson-Dans, Andrew Thomson, Margaret Thomson

Where is it? *9 km south of Perth via Canning Highway and Point Walter Road.*
Travelling time: *20 minutes from Perth.*
Facilities: *Lookouts, BBQs, kiosk, cafe, playground, toilets, carpark, bike racks, safe swimming beach.*
On-site information: *Information panels.*
Best season: *All year.*

MARRI

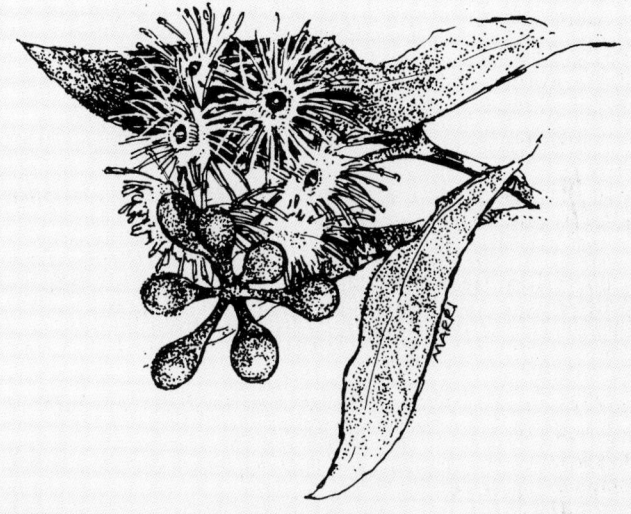

This majestic, spreading tree is one of the most common trees of the South West forests. Marri belongs to a group of trees known as bloodwoods, because their trunks exude a dark red gum. The gum, or kino, was ingested by Aboriginal people for medicinal purposes. The bloodwoods were once considered to be eucalypts but were recently placed in a separate genus, *Corymbia*. Marri's specific name *calophylla* celebrates its beautiful leaves, which are dull to shiny dark green above and paler below, with closely-packed veins.

The large woody urn-shaped fruits of marri are known as honkey nuts, and inspired May Gibbs' stories about the gumnut babies, Snugglepot and Cuddlepie. Marri has the largest seeds of any eucalypt and is a very important food source for a range of parrots and cockatoos.

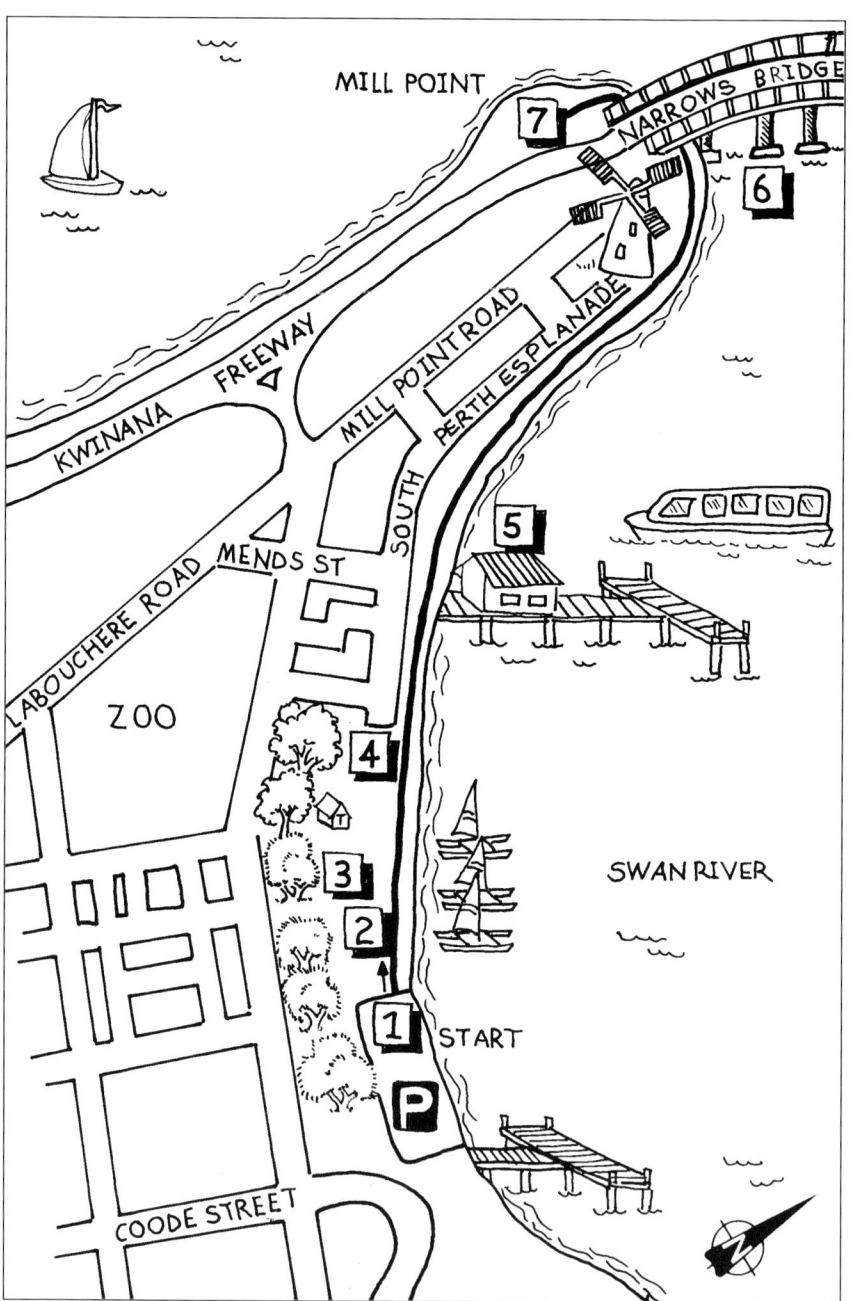

MILL POINT

NARROWS BRIDGE

7

6

KWINANA FREEWAY

MILL POINT ROAD

SOUTH PERTH ESPLANADE

5

LABOUCHERE ROAD

MENDS ST

ZOO

4

SWAN RIVER

3

2

1 START

P

COODE STREET

South Perth Foreshore Walk

36

Length: *3.5 km return.*
Class: *1.*
Walk time: *1 hour, 20 minutes.*

This walk provides excellent views across Perth Water to the city and, near the end of the walk, across Melville Water to Kings Park and Matilda Bay.

1   Starting at the carpark at the foreshore end of Coode Street, you will find picnic shelters from which there are good views of the city. Catamarans can be hired during the summer months. Walk west from here.

2   A few minutes along the walk is a plaque commemorating the re-enactment of Sir James Stirling's landing.

3   A swampy area of paperbark trees, with a raised, timber-decked walkway, can be seen to your left.

4   You will pass toilets, a playground and scented gardens.

5   Next is a ferry jetty which services Barrack Street.

6   The Old Mill, by the side of the freeway on Point Belches, is the oldest surviving physical link with the pioneering days of the Swan River Colony. It was built by William Kernot Shenton and, together with the site and surrounding outbuildings, was declared a State Public Recreation Reserve in 1932. A small fee is charged to enter the Old Mill (check opening times).

7   Continue along the river's edge and under the Narrows Bridge to Mill Point. From here, there are good views of Kings Park, the Old Swan Brewery, the Royal Perth Yacht Club in Matilda Bay and the South Perth Yacht Club near the Canning River. At weekends, Melville Water is a mass of colourful sails and spinnakers. During summer, parasailing and waterskiing are available from Mill Point. Return to the start along the same route.

Ray Bailey, Gil Masters

Where is it? *Northern end of Coode Street, South Perth.*
Travelling time: *10 minutes from Perth.*
Facilities: *Picnic tables at start of walk; restaurants, cafes and shops in Mends Street; toilets and playground en route.*
Best season: *All year. Summer for catamarans, parasailing and waterskiing.*

The South Walks 37 – 48

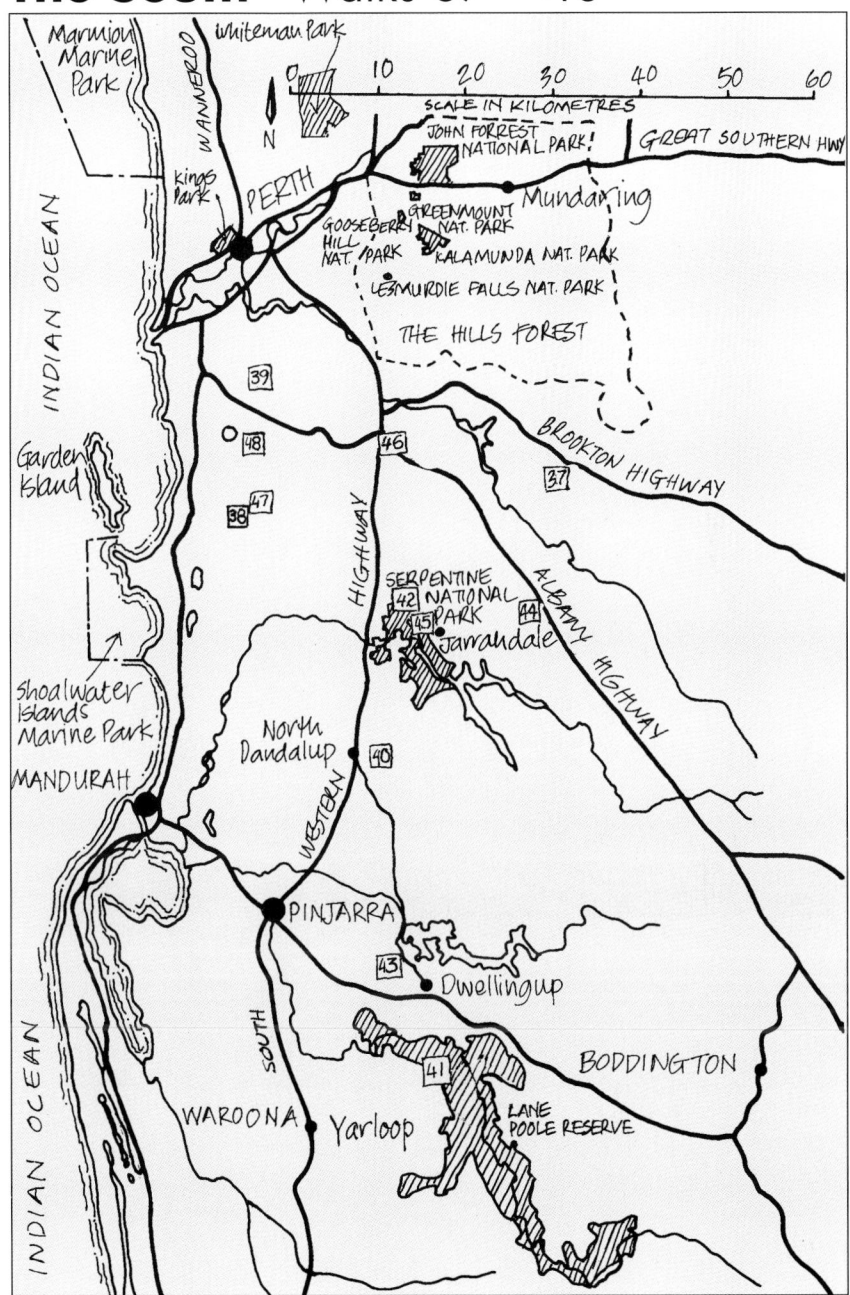

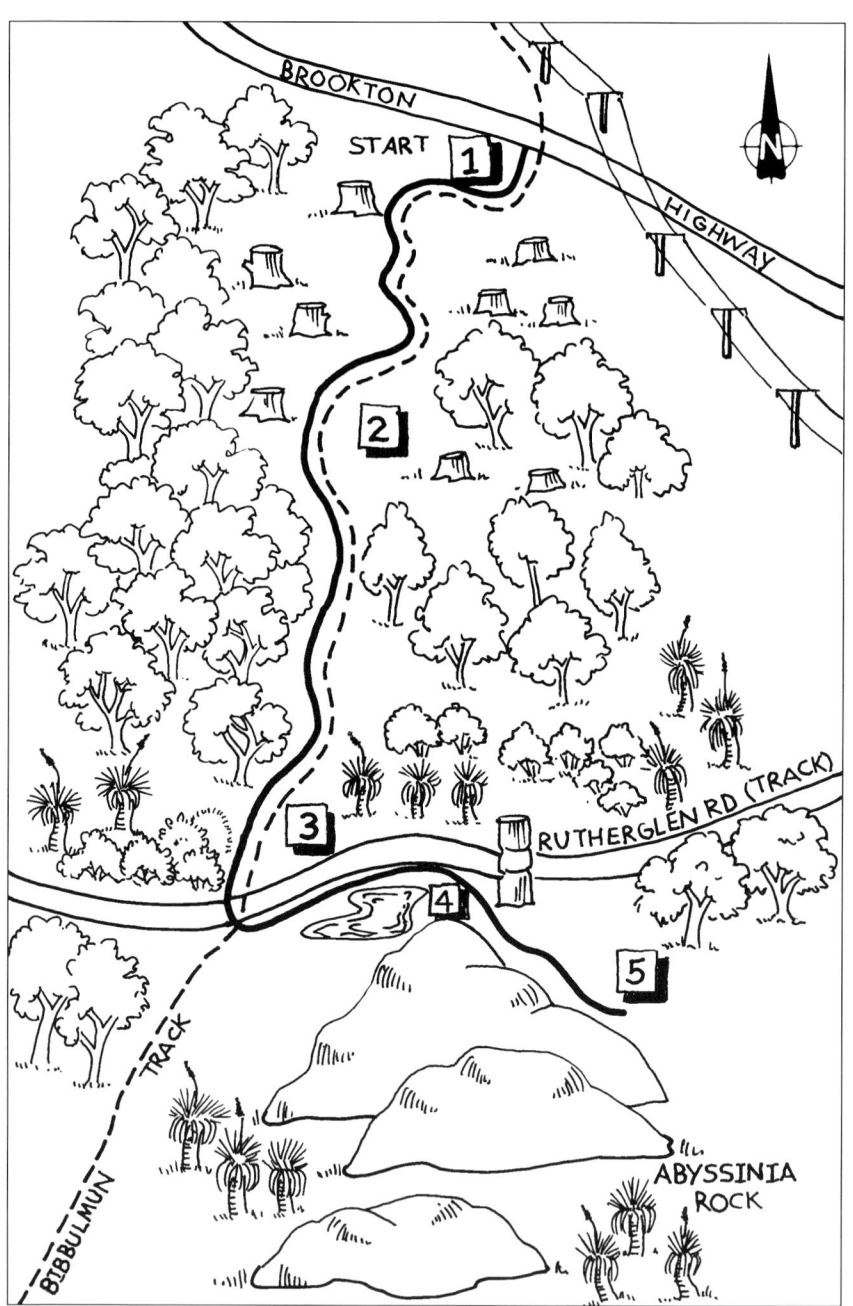

Length: *12 km return.*
Class: *4.*
Walk time: *5-6 hours.*

This trail features jarrah woodlands, with thickets of teatree and flooded gum in the gullies, and leads to a large granite outcrop that supports a variety of plant life. Take time to explore the rock, on which lizards may be sunning themselves. Take care not to stand on the sensitive mosses as they are very slow to regenerate. Much of this walk is through a Disease Risk Area, which is quarantined to help prevent the introduction and spread of dieback disease. Please ensure your boots or shoes are clean and please do not stray from the track.

1   Start at the intersection between the Brookton Highway and the Bibbulmun Track (look for a powerline crossing the highway). Follow the Bibbulmun Track markers (yellow triangles with a Waugal symbol) south.
2   Meander down to the first gully. Along this section you will see evidence of logging and firewood cutting. Much of the bush has been thinned to promote growth and to establish regeneration (jarrah and marri seedlings).
3   The vegetation changes from jarrah woodland to a scrubby heathland. This lower valley becomes too moist during the winter months for jarrah and marri to survive. Turn left at the T-junction.
4   You will see a waterhole, which was built to provide water for fire-fighting. This type of woodland is very flammable and care must be taken when lighting a campfire or disposing of cigarette butts. A little further along, turn right at the totem sign. Follow the track up to Abyssinia Rock.
5   Abyssinia Rock contains a variety of plant life, ranging from small mosses and liverworts to hakea shrubs and large sheoaks.

Andy Darbyshire, Peter Gibson, Jamie Ridley

Where is it? *60 km south-east of Perth along Brookton Highway.*
Travelling time: *1 hour.*
Facilities: *Carpark at start.*
On-site information: *Yellow Bibbulmun Track markers.*
Best season: *All year except after rain when ground is wet.*

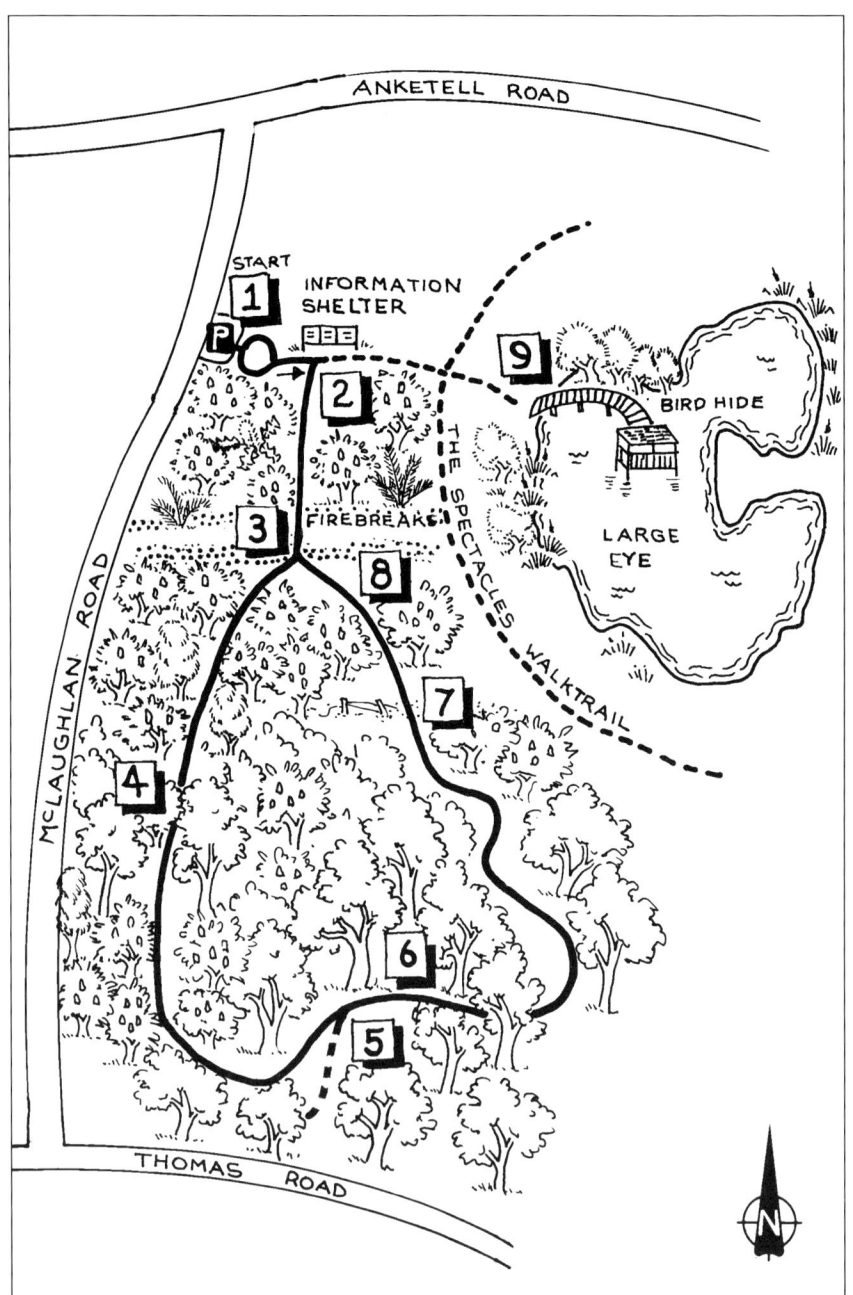

Banksia Woodland Trail   **38**

Beeliar Regional Park

Length: *3 km loop.*
Class: *3 (not suitable for wheelchairs or strollers).*
Walk time: *50 minutes.*

The Banksia Woodland Trail is an alternative experience to The Spectacles Walktrail. It traverses remnant coastal woodlands of banksia and jarrah.

1   Begin at the McLaughlan Road parking area at The Spectacles, a 360 hectare wetland area protected in the Beeliar Regional Park.
2   Just after passing through the gate, you will see an information shelter and the trailhead sign. Ignoring the main path straight ahead, turn right into the Banksia Woodland Trail, into woodlands of candle banksia and firewood banksia. Occasional holly-leaf banksias (*Banksia ilicifolia*), primitive banksias with close links to the dryandras and which greatly resemble parrotbush, grow alongside the trail. They have short holly-like leaves and small domed flower clusters which change colour when pollinated from yellow to pinkish-red, signalling to visiting birds and insects that nectar and pollen are found only in the yellow flowers.
3   Cross a firebreak, then another one, after which the track diverges. Take the right hand trail. There are numerous sheoak (*Allocasuarina fraseriana*) trees. There is a lot of evidence of frequent fires, such as blackened trees and an undergrowth which as been taken over by veldt grass.
4   Jarrah trees begin to appear, recognised by the vertical grooves in their rough greyish-brown fibrous bark, along with scattered grasstrees.
5   A track heads to the right. Ignore it and continue along the trail.
6   The woodland becomes more open and there are a few large jarrah trees which are noticeably taller than the surounding vegetation, mainly banksias.
7   Cross an overgrown firebreak next to an old fence.
8   After reaching the firebreak at point 3, return to the information shelter.
9   Turn right at the information shelter to check out the Biara Bird Hide, an optional 800 metre return walk.

Carolyn Thomson-Dans

Where is it? *31 km from Perth.*
Travelling time: *40 minutes from Perth via the Kwinana Freeway and Anketell Rd.*
Facilities: *Nearby bird hide.*
On-site information: *Information shelter, trailhead sign.*
Best season: *Spring for wildflowers.*

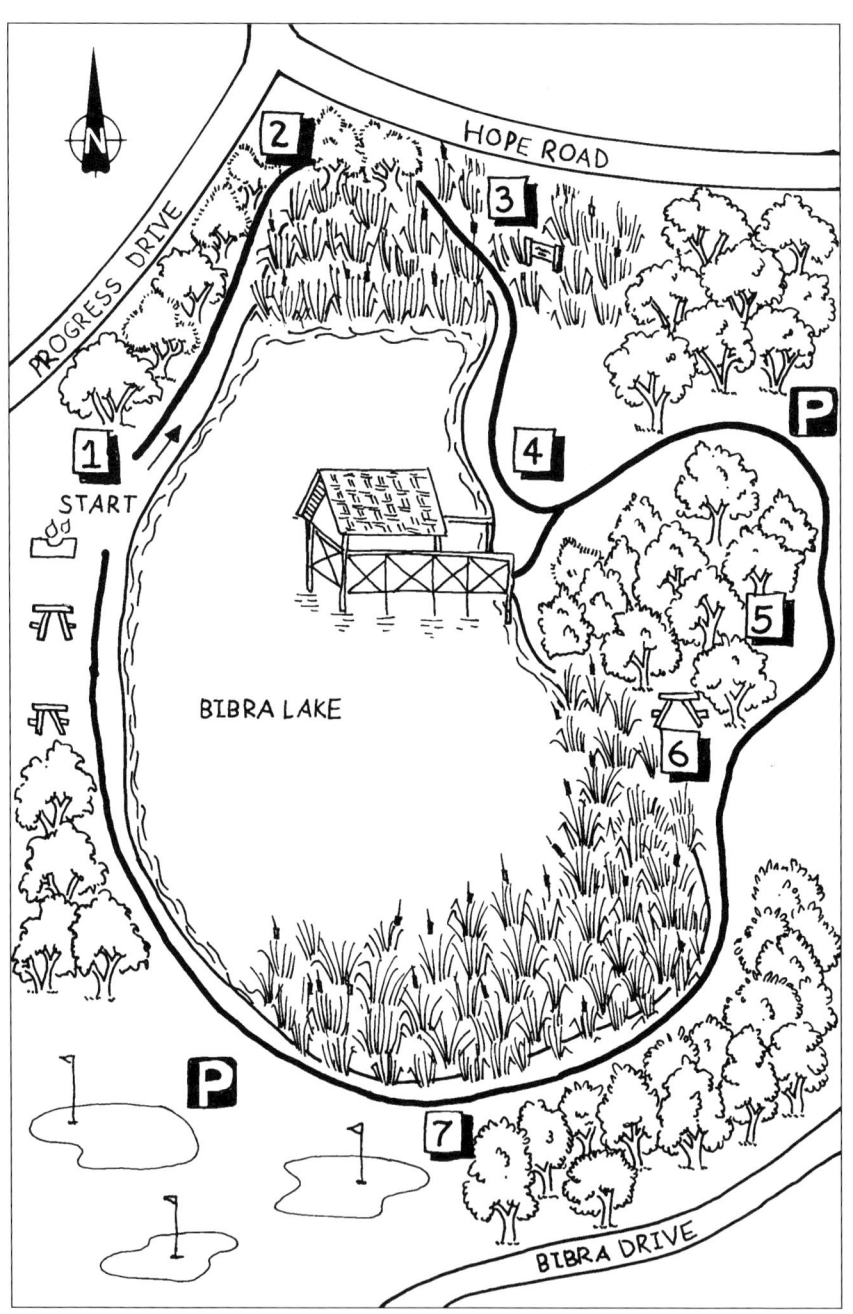

140

Bibra Lake Walk

39

Beeliar Regional Park

Length: *6 km loop.*
Class: *1.*
Walk time: *2 hours.*

Bibra Lake and its surrounds are an outstanding refuge for birds. Waterbirds, including occasional spoonbills, inhabit the lake and surrounding reed beds. On the western side of the lake there are many semi-tame birds, including black swans, coots, purple swamphens and ducks. The paperbarks, flooded gums and adjoining bush vegetation attract many bush birds. The dual-use walk/cycle track is suitable for wheelchairs, prams and strollers.

1 Starting at the picnic area, the first part of the walk traverses a grassed area with some paperbarks and flooded gums.
2 The reed beds become thicker and the paperbarks hang over the path, forming a tunnel.
3 Signs indicate the presence of snakes. Walkers should beware of snakes when walking in or near any wetland or native bush area.
4 At the end of a wooden pier, well beyond the fringing paperbarks, a bird hide allows you to watch waterbirds and waders. After heavy rains, the lake's water level rises and can make the hide inaccessible.
5 The path skirts around a large area of old cultivation, which has reverted to introduced grasses and a selection of planted native trees and shrubs. This area attracts a wide variety of birds, including the chestnut-breasted mannikin, a species not usually found in the South West.
6 As the path winds back to the lakeside, there is a small picnic area where you can relax and observe the wildlife.
7 This section, running back to the main picnic area, has been grassed and planted with ornamental trees.

Stacey Strickland, Annabelle Vowels

Where is it? *18 km south of Perth on Progress Drive.*
Travelling time: *30 minutes via Kwinana Freeway and Hope Road.*
Facilities: *BBQs, playground, carparks, toilets.*
Best season: *Spring, summer, early autumn.*

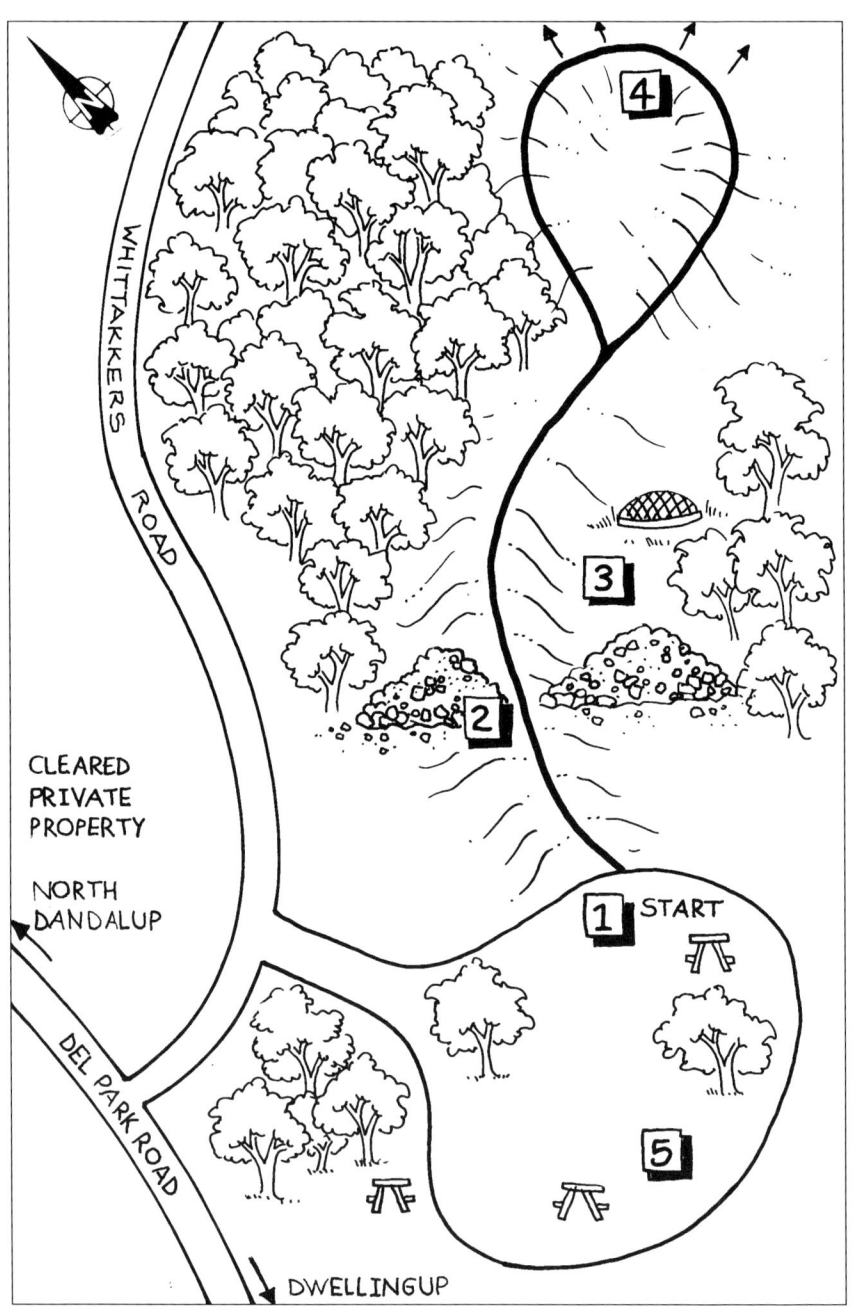

WHITTAKKERS ROAD

CLEARED
PRIVATE
PROPERTY

NORTH
DANDALUP

DEL PARK ROAD

DWELLINGUP

4

3

2

1 START

5

Goldmine Hill Walk

40

Length: *400 m return.*
Class: *2.*
Walk time: *10 minutes.*

Although this is quite a short walk, it has been included because of its interesting features and proximity to the popular Goldmine Hill picnic site. It affords good views of the Peel Inlet and Swan Coastal Plain. The diverse vegetation along the walk includes salmon white gum, wandoo and dwarf mountain marri.

1   Begin at the trailhead sign, on the north-eastern side of the carpark. The trail leads up a steep, slippery incline.
2   A mullock heap shows the different rocks that were excavated from the mineshaft as miners dug for gold.
3   A mineshaft, covered by a grill, is approximately 7.5 metres deep. No gold was found in the area.
4   There is a lookout, with good views of the Peel Inlet and Swan Coastal Plain.
5   You soon reach a picnic area. It is good for fossicking, with evidence of prospecting.

John Hanel, Mark Humble

Where is it? *65 km south of Perth via South-West Highway, Del Park Road and Whittaker Road.*
Travelling time: *1 hour, 30 minutes.*
Facilities: *BBQs and carpark.*
On-site information: *Trailhead sign.*
Best season: *All year.*

King Jarrah Track

Lane Poole Reserve

41

Length: *18 km loop.*
Class: *3.*
Walk time: *5 hours.*

The highlight of this walk is the king jarrah (*Eucalyptus marginata*), a majestic 250-year-old tree. Much of the track runs along the Murray River. There is a campsite roughly mid-way along the track for those wishing to take their time and make a weekend of the walk. The Munda Biddi Bike Trail follows some of this walk, so walkers may encounter bikes.

1 The track begins at the old Nanga Mill townsite. A campsite has now been established there in a grove of tall pines.
2 A detour off the track takes you to the Stringers, a small picnic and camping site by the Murray River with canoe launching facilities and swimming holes. Some old bridge stringers are visible in the water.
3 There is an old logging railway formation with cuttings and old bridge sites.
4 Various reference trees can be seen. These numbered trees allow foresters to accurately locate their position in the bush.
5 The remains of an old railway bridge can be seen.
6 There is a campsite with barbecue rings and a toilet about 200 metres off the track to the south.
7 A log bridge takes you over Big Brook.
8 The king jarrah tree is the next point of interest.
9 Dawn Creek has good water in winter and spring.
10 A very large, old axe and crosscut stump with evidence of board notches is visible here.
11 A large burnt-out, hollow jarrah tree.
12 The track skirts a large dieback-infected area. Some trees along the track have been blown over, exposing the underlying rock.
13 The track passes through dense prickly thickets of waterbush.
14 Christmas Creek is a small seasonal creek. Birdsong and frog calls can be heard at appropriate times of the year.
15 You will reach an even-aged regrowth forest with numerous large stumps and old logging debris.
16 A very colourful acacia grows here and flowers in the spring.

17 Just before returning to Nanga Mill, the trail passes through a badly affected dieback area.

Matthew Reynolds, Mark Humble

Where is it? *Nanga Mill is 13 km south of Dwellingup along Nanga Road.*
Travelling time: *2 hours, 30 minutes from Perth.*
Facilities: *BBQs, tables, toilets, campsite.*
On-site information: *Signs on access road and at trailhead, yellow markers along the route.*
Best season: *Spring for wildflowers, summer.*

JARRAH

The jarrah forest extends from the South Coast almost to New Norcia, about 125 kilometres north of Perth. It is bounded to the east by the line of annual rainfall of about 600 millimetres. In the northern part of its range it is found on laterite soils of the Darling Range and occasionally in the sandy soils of the coastal plain.

Jarrah *(Eucalyptus marginata)* has dark grey or reddish-brown bark with deep vertical grooves. It grows to about 40 metres tall on the richest and best watered soils of the Darling Range, but seldom reaches more than 15 metres on poorer sandy soils.

Jarrah forms extensive forests with marri and other trees. In forest areas, jarrah trees grow about 0.5 centimetres in diameter each year and can live for more than 400 years. The trees are generally widely spaced, with an open crown allowing light to pass through to the forest floor. It is a beautiful forest all year round, but particularly during the spring, when its understorey of shrubs and herbs bursts into flower.

Jarrah is a good honey-yielding species and jarrah pollen is considered to be highly nutritious. The jarrah forests and coastal stands yield fairly large quantities of a medium amber, nutty-flavoured honey.

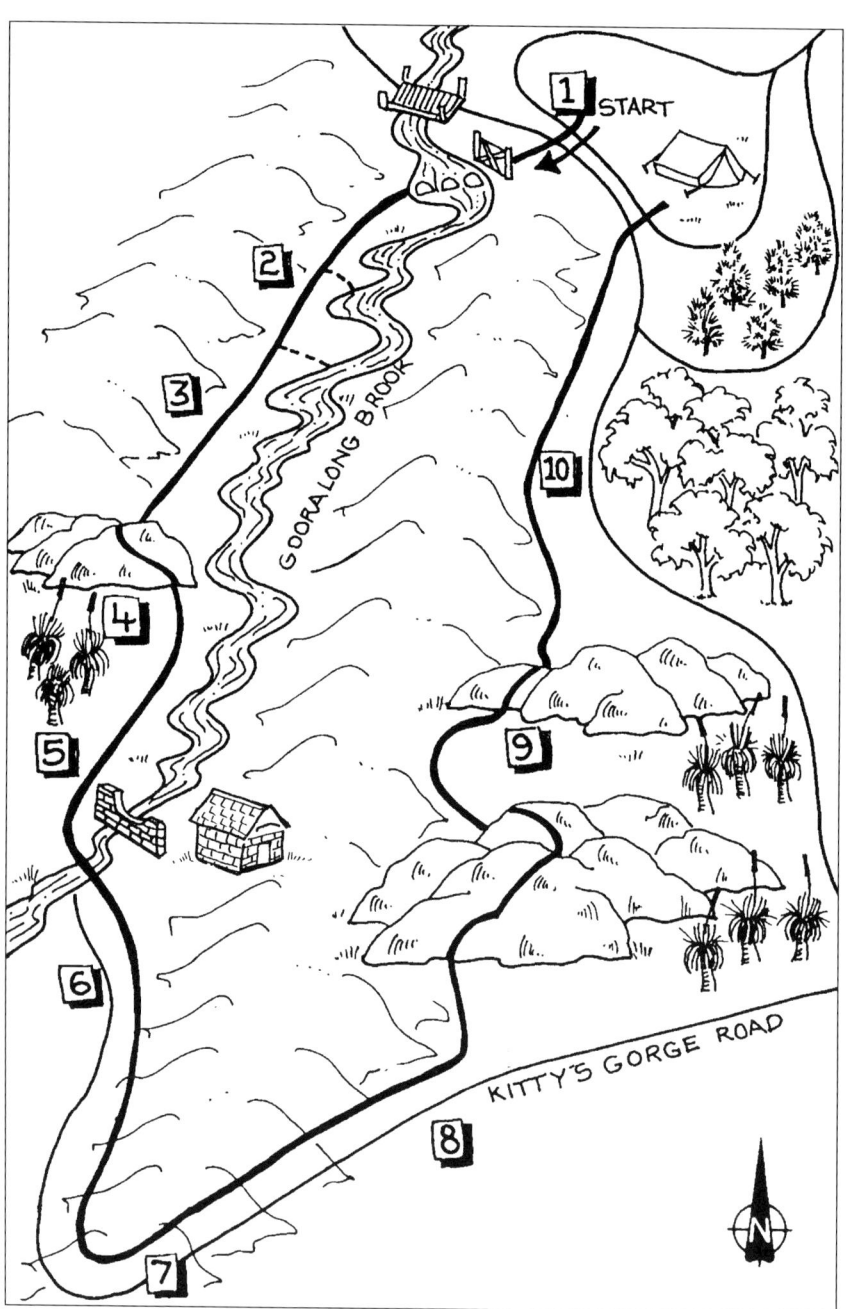

Kitty's Track

42

Length: *4.5 km loop.*
Class: *4.*
Walk time: *2 hours.*

This walk passes down the Darling Scarp into the Gooralong Brook valley to a gauging station. It returns along the brook and through jarrah forest, giving views to the ocean. It also features interesting vegetation on the granite slopes.

1 Starting from the carpark, cross the bridge at Gooralong Brook. The brook flows all year round. From here, head south on the western side of the brook.
2 About 200 metres from the start of the walk, several side tracks lead down to the brook, giving pleasant views of the pools.
3 Occasional gullies occur, with water flowing over the track only during winter.
4 Granite outcrops are visible on both sides of the brook. The stunted flora in these areas has adapted to the poor soil and harsh conditions.
5 You will see a water gauging station. This weir and wall is an active measuring site for water quality and quantity. Cross the brook at this point.
6 Continue south, on the eastern side of the brook, along the weir access track.
7 After about 1.5 kilometres, the track swings to the east and then north. Follow the directional markers to the top of the ridge.
8 Leave the access track and head north along the top of the ridge, following the markers.
9 Winding through the bush, you will have excellent views to the ocean around Mandurah.
10 Continue until you arrive at another track. Turn left and head for the Gooralong Pine Plantation.
11 When you reach the Pine Plantation, walk downhill to the carpark and picnic facilities.

Andy Darbyshire, Jamie Ridley

Where is it? *Gooralong is 50 km south of Perth via Jarrahdale.*
Travelling time: *1 hour, 10 minutes from Perth.*
Facilities: *BBQs, carpark, toilets.*
On-site information: *Display shelter at Gooralong, markers along track.*
Best season: *Spring for wildflowers.*

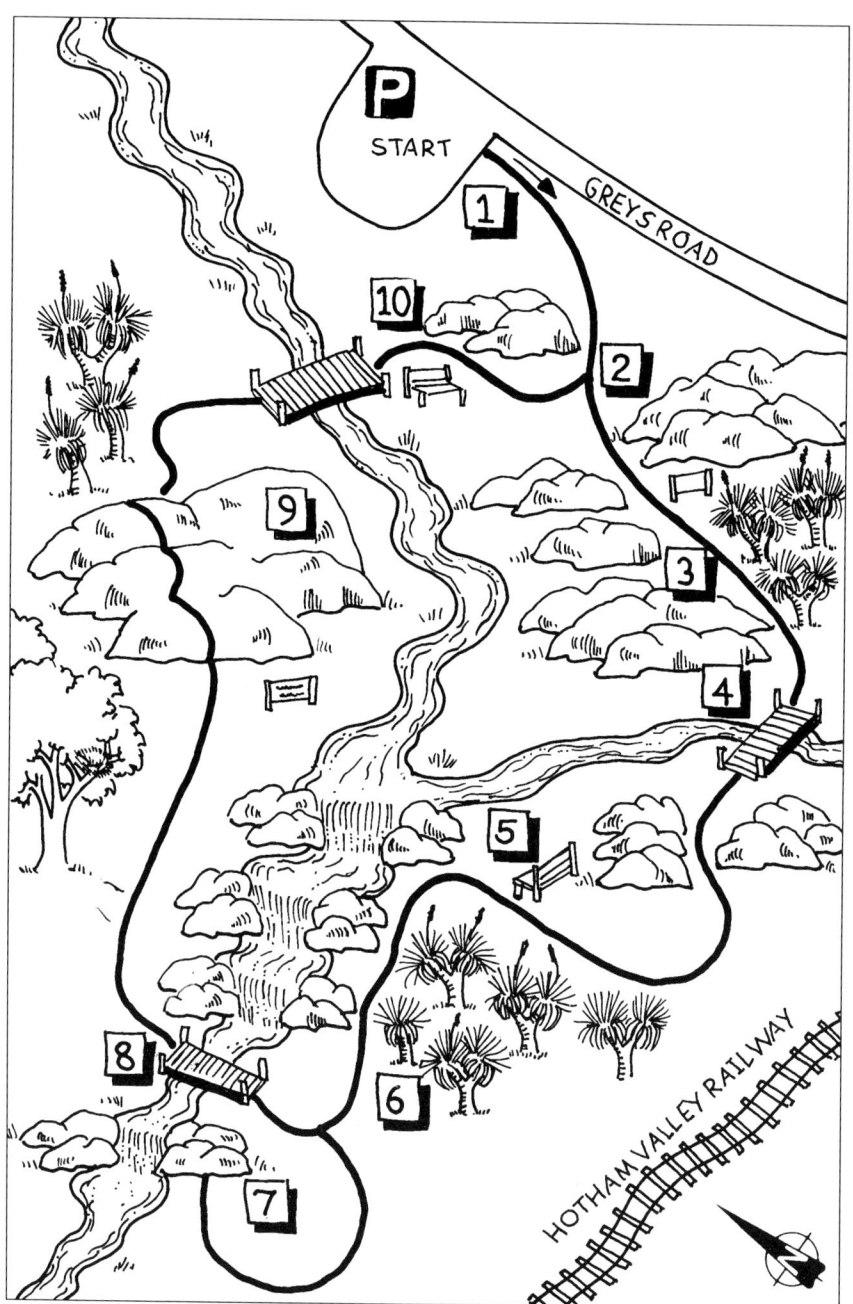

Marrinup Falls Walktrail

43

Length: *1.5 km loop.*
Class: *2.*
Walk time: *45 minutes.*

This walk, through a variety of vegetation, takes you along Marrinup Brook to the falls, returning on the opposite bank.

1 The trail begins at the southern end of the carpark.
2 At the junction of the return loop, to the left of the trail, there is a large granite outcrop covered in moss, lichen and fungi. Looking west, you may see a wedge-tailed eagle's nest in the trees on the top of the hill.
3 The trail winds down over rocks and past an interpretive sign to Marrinup Brook. There are many large, multi-headed grasstrees in this area.
4 Cross Marrinup Brook over a small log bridge and turn right towards the falls.
5 A seat is provided along this section. The trail then passes a series of waterfalls before reaching the junction with the return loop.
6 At this point, a spur to the main falls leads off to the left.
7 Enjoy the main falls and pool. Brown quail can sometimes be seen here. Return to point 6 and turn left along the return loop.
8 Cross Marrinup Brook by means of a small log footbridge.
9 The track climbs uphill, past interpretive signs, and crosses a large granite outcrop before turning right to an unnamed creek.
10 A small causeway crosses the creek. There is a log seat on which you can rest for a while. Head back up to join the outward loop at point 2, then turn left towards the carpark.

John Hanel, Mark Humble

Where is it? *100 km south of Perth via Williams Road, west of Dwellingup, and Grey Road.*
Travelling time: *2 hours, 15 minutes.*
Facilities: *Carpark. There is a tavern, petrol and so on in Dwellingup.*
On-site information: *Interpretive signs along the route.*
Best season: *All year, winter and spring for waterfalls and wildflowers.*

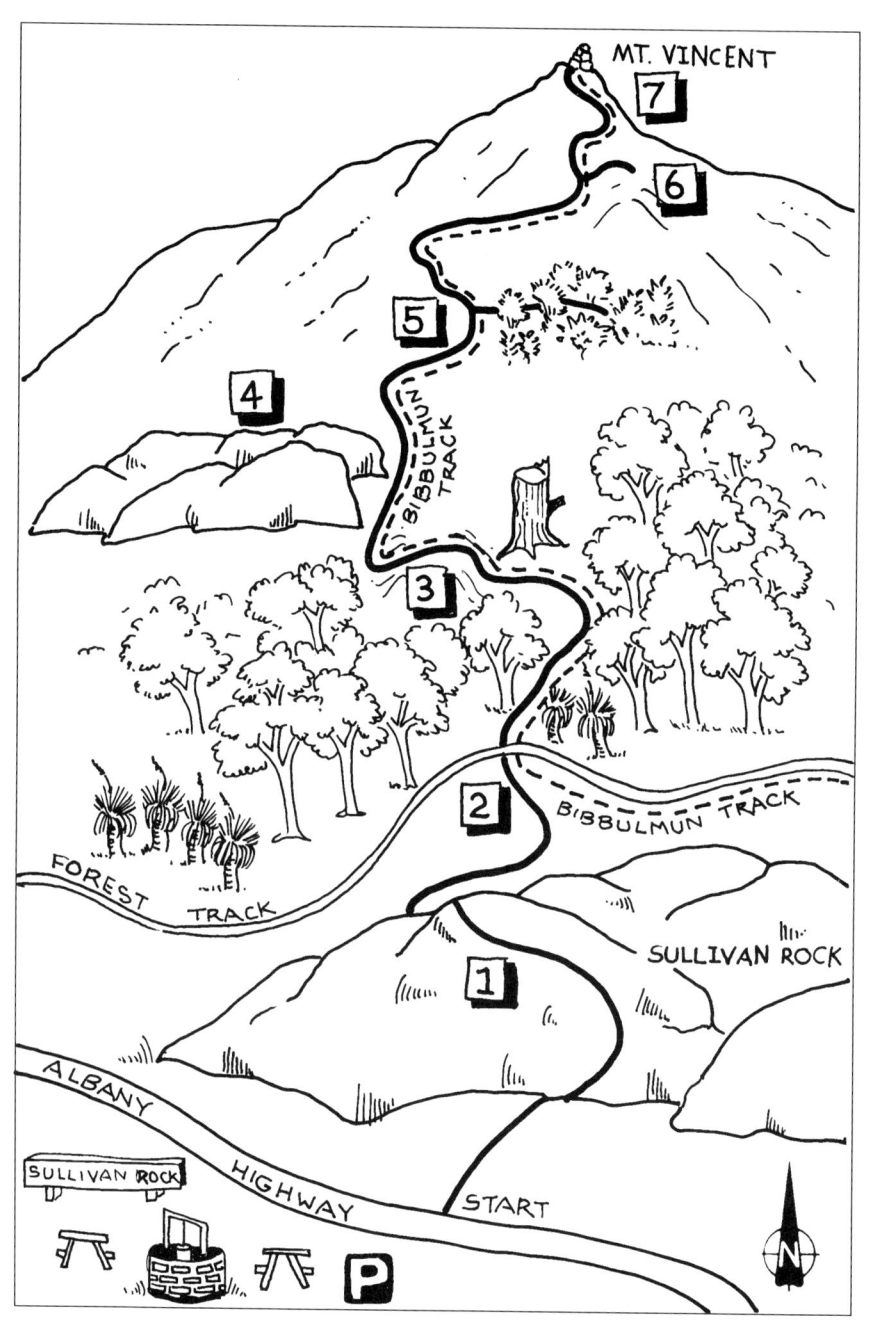

Mt Vincent Walktrail via Sullivan Rock

44

Monadnocks Conservation Park

Length: *7 km return.*
Class: *4-5.*
Walk time: *2 hours, 30 minutes.*

This trail follows the Bibbulmun Track to the summit of Mt Vincent and features scenic views and granite outcrops, called 'monadnocks' by local Aboriginal people. It is particularly rewarding during the wildflower season. Many birds can be seen: ravens and grey currawongs near the highway; scarlet robins, grey fantails and splendid fairy-wrens in the forest; and wedge-tailed eagles in the sky above Mt Vincent.

1 After parking at the picnic area, cross Albany Highway following the Bibbulmun Track up Sullivan Rock. Pegs set into the rock mark the trail and should be strictly followed. A variety of plant life grows on the rock and much of it is sensitive. If walked on, most of the plants will die. Mt Cooke can be seen to the south-east.

2 From Sullivan Rock, continue to follow the Bibbulmun Track (yellow markers) into an area of mature jarrah and marri forest.

3 As you cross the small ridge you will see many old stumps of trees cut by axe and cross-cut saw. On the right is a stump that still has an original peg in it.

4 The track runs to the right of a large granite outcrop.

5 Here, the track passes through a thick stand of hakeas and is partly overgrown. At the fork, take the lower track. If you look at the horizon to the north-west you can just see Alcoa's Jarrahdale mine clearing.

6 To the east, there is a small lookout on a spur track. Yellow direction markers are fixed to a tree at this point. Take the left hand track.

7 At the summit there is a cairn (pile of rocks). Looking north you can see Mt Cuthbert and slightly east on the horizon is Mt Dale. Retrace your steps to the picnic area.

Ken Wheeler, Grant Hansen, Jamie Ridley

Where is it? *Sullivan Rock, 65 km south of Perth on Albany Highway.*
Travelling time: *1 hour, 30 minutes.*
Facilities: *Picnic area, BBQ, carpark.*
On-site information: *Trailhead sign, some markers along route.*
Best season: *Autumn, winter, spring for wildflowers.*

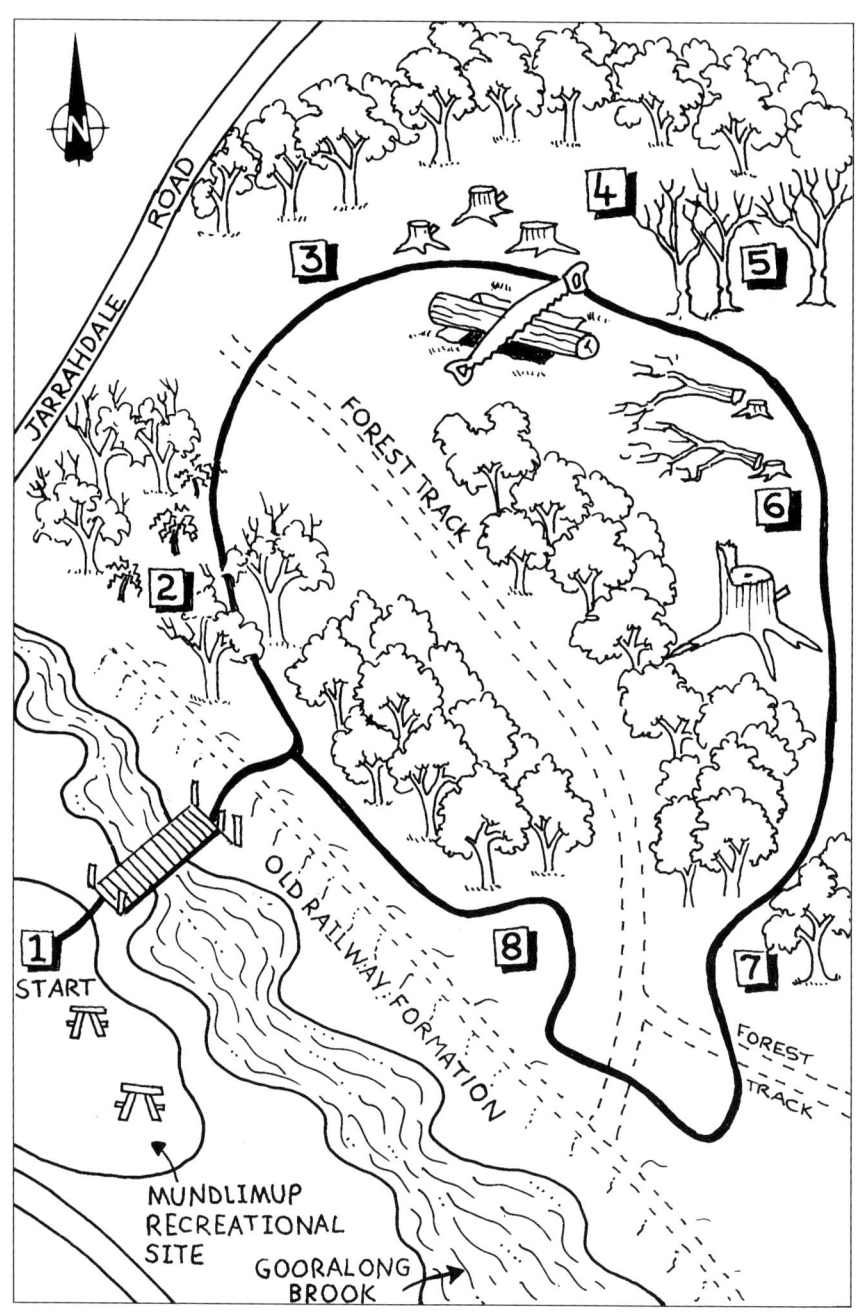

N

JARRAHDALE ROAD

3

4

5

FOREST TRACK

2

6

1
START

OLD RAILWAY FORMATION

8

7

FOREST TRACK

MUNDLIMUP
RECREATIONAL
SITE

GOORALONG
BROOK

Mundlimup Trail

Length: *3.2 km loop.*
Class: *3.*
Walk time: *1 hour.*

This trail features a history of logging and silviculture, and passes through a fine example of northern jarrah forest.

1   From the Mundlimup Recreation Site, cross the bridge over the creek to an old railway formation. Turn right, proceed about 50 metres, and then turn left.
2   About 100 metres from the railway formation, you will see a small dieback-infected area. Here, you can see the devastation wrought by the disease. Fresh banksia and jarrah deaths may be evident.
3   On this part of the trail you will see evidence of old logging operations.
4   This old sawpit was used prior to the 1950s for milling logs. Using a two-handed saw, one man stood on top of a log while another stood in the pit beneath, and together they sawed rough planks of wood, a primitive method by today's standards.
5   Crossing a forest track, you will see old trees that have been ringbarked. This was a method used to kill non-viable trees and hence promote the growth of more valuable crop trees.
6   A little further on, you will see a large stump with a trail marker attached. The tree was felled with axe and crosscut saw. Often, trees were cut high to reduce the diameter and/or to get above any defects. To cut a tree high up, axemen stood on pegs attached to the sides of the tree. The notches that would have taken such pegs can still be seen in the stump.
7   Follow the forest track for a few hundred metres, then branch off to the left through more open jarrah woodland, keeping an eye open for the trail markers.
8   The track rejoins the old railway formation. Follow this back to the recreation site.

Peter Gibson, Jamie Ridley

Where is it? *55 km south of Perth via Jarrahdale Road and Balmoral Road.*
Travelling time: *1 hour from Perth.*
Facilities: *BBQs, carpark.*
On-site information: *Directional signs along the trail.*
Best season: *Autumn, spring for wildflowers.*

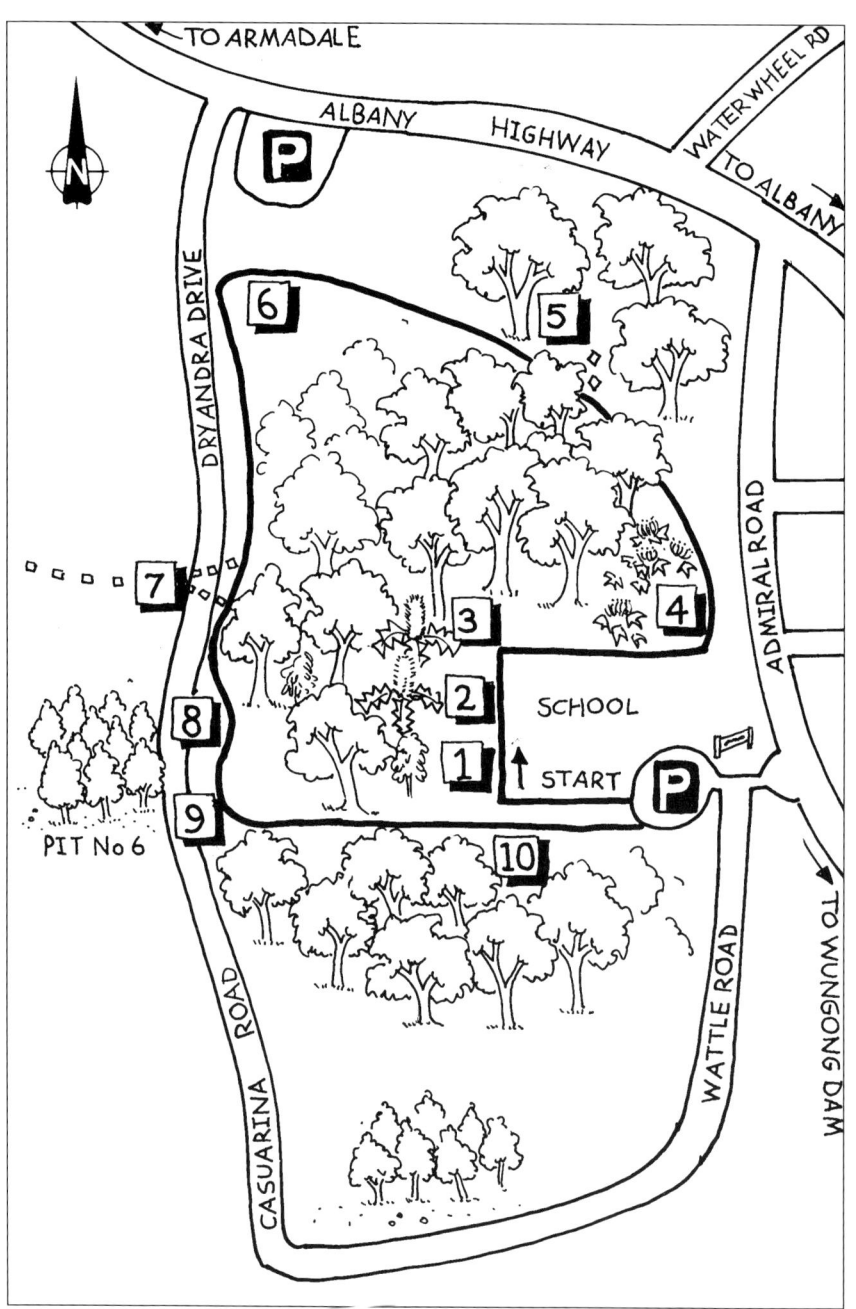

TO ARMADALE

WATER WHEEL RD

ALBANY HIGHWAY

TO ALBANY

N

P

DRYANDRA DRIVE

6

5

7

3

4

ADMIRAL ROAD

8

2

9

1

SCHOOL

START

P

PIT No 6

10

CASUARINA ROAD

WATTLE ROAD

TO WUNGONG DAM

156

Robin Ramble

46

Bungendore Park

Length: *3 km loop.*
Class: *3.*
Walk time: *1 hour, 30 minutes.*

This is one in a series of walks in Bungendore Park near Armadale. The walk winds through sheoak trees and dense stands of parrotbush, where western spinebills and New Holland honeyeaters search for nectar.

1   Begin at the carpark just south of Armadale Christian School. Follow the yellow dots, which have a bird symbol, into jarrah woodland.
2   There is an interpretive totem by the side of the trail. Snottygobbles (*Persoonia* species) and bull banksias (*Banksia grandis*) grow nearby.
3   At the junction with Spinebill Stroll (marked by red squares), the vegetation changes to sheoaks.
4   Turn left into an area of parrotbush (*Dryandra sessilis*).
5   Red diamonds mark the junction with the Whistler Walk.
6   At the junction with Dryandra Drive many grevilleas and hibbertias can be seen.
7   There are open views at the junction with Honeyeater Hike (marked by yellow squares).
8   The rehabilitation project at gravel pit No. 6 began in June 1987. Parrotbush has revegetated naturally, whereas marri and other trees have been planted.
9   After reaching the junction of Dryandra Drive, Casuarina Road and Spinebill Stroll, turn left and head east.
10 Return to the carpark.

Terry Hales

Where is it? *31 km from Perth off Admiral Road.*
Travelling time: *1 hour, 10 minutes from Perth via Albany Highway.*
Facilities: *Carpark.*
On-site information: *Signs on access road, at trailhead and along trail.*
Best season: *Autumn, winter, spring for wildflowers.*

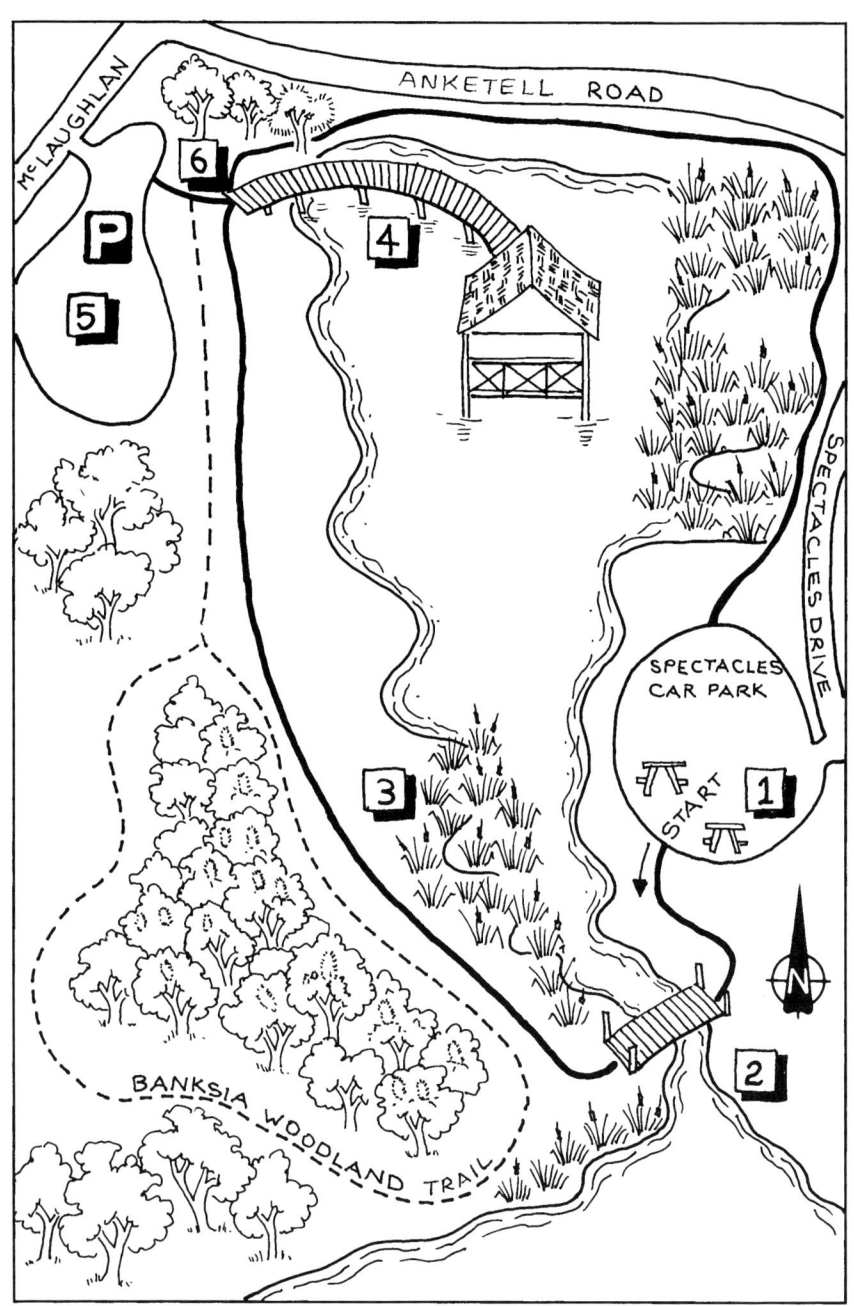

The Spectacles Walktrail

47

Beeliar Regional Park

Length: *5 km return.*
Class: *2 (accessible by wheelchair).*
Walk time: *2 hours.*

This walktrail is part of a joint CALM-Alcoa project in this important wetland area. The Spectacles is so-named because of the shape of its two wetlands when viewed from the air. The area was once part of the original Peel Settlement Scheme of the 1920s. It features paperbark groves, banksia woodland, wildflowers (in season) and a 100 metre boardwalk to a bird hide.

1   The Spectacles Drive Picnic Area overlooks reed beds and open water.
2   A bridge over the channel links the two 'eyes' of The Spectacles. Water flows all year and the area attracts birds, frogs, insects and reptiles. There is a bench and rest area.
3   The valley. This largely open area is being revegetated. This is a transition zone between the woodland and wetland, and the trail winds through both. Banksias, eucalypts and understorey plants such as the succulent pigface can be seen.
4   A boardwalk through pleasant enclosed paperbark wetland takes you to the Biara Bird Hide over open water. You may see birds, insects, the occasional snake and other reptiles and amphibians.
5   At the McLaughlan Road entrance there is a carpark and trailhead information shelter set in banksia woodland. Return to the Spectacles Drive Picnic Area.
6   The trail heads north around the 'Large Eye' and returns to the Spectacles Drive Picnic Area.

Richard Hammond, Annabelle Vowels

Where is it? *31 km from Perth on Spectacles Drive.*
Travelling time: *40 minutes from Perth via the Kwinana Freeway and Anketell Road.*
Facilities: *Picnic tables, carpark.*
On-site information: *Trailhead signs, information shelter.*
Best season: *All year, spring for wildflowers.*

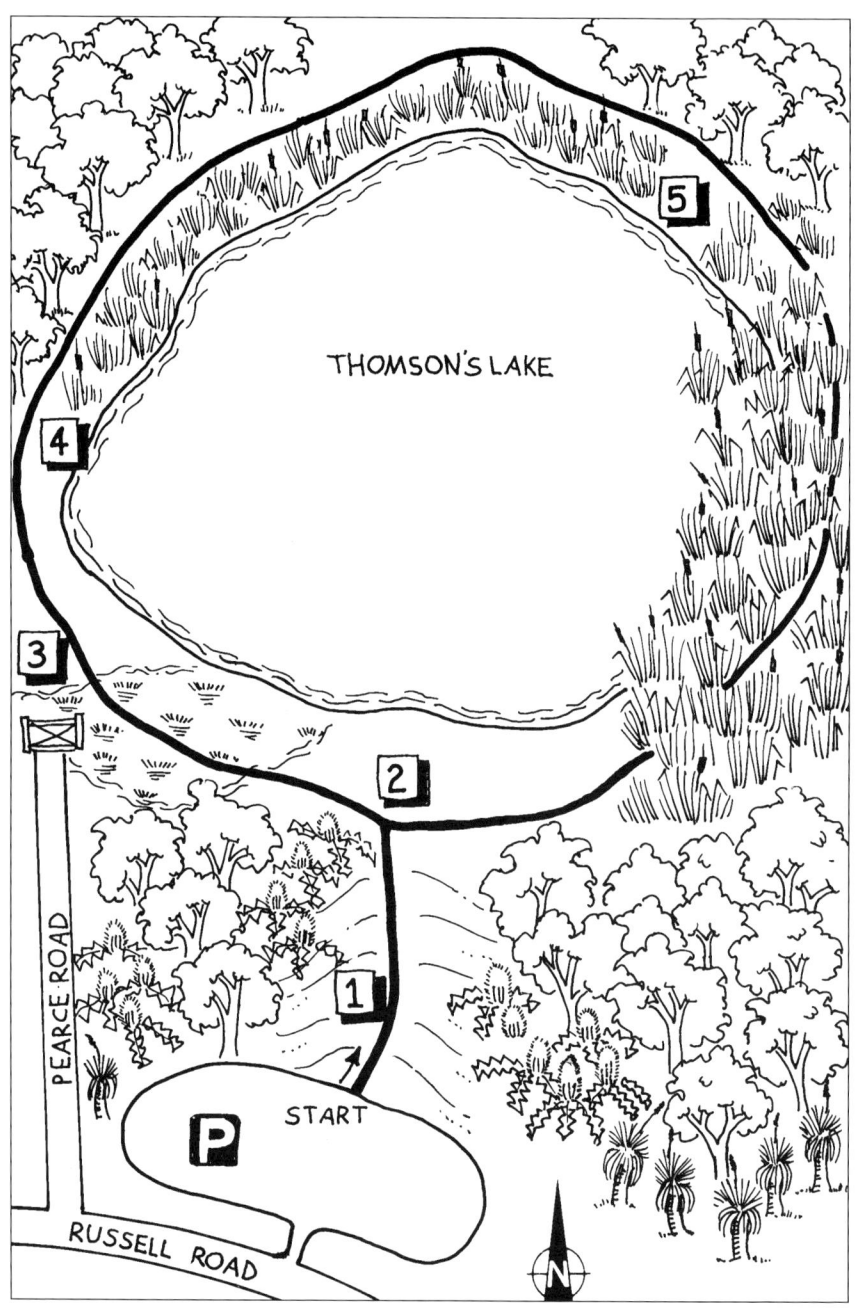

THOMSON'S LAKE

5

4

3

2

1

START

P

PEARCE ROAD

RUSSELL ROAD

N

Thomsons Lake Trail 48

Beeliar Regional Park

Length: *5.7 km loop.*
Class: *3-4.*
Walk time: *3 hours.*

Bulrushes, birds and the wetlands environment are the hallmarks of this walk. Thomsons Lake is an important area for migratory waterbirds, especially waders. In winter there are more birds on the wetland, but parts of the trail become water-logged. In summer the trail is drier and more accessible, but take care as snakes are more abundant.

1   From the crest of the ridge, a few metres from the carpark, there are excellent views across the lake and the nearby jarrah and banksia woodland.
2   At the T-junction, turn left and proceed around the lake in a clockwise direction. Bulrushes crowd along the edge of the lake and there are partial views of the water.
3   The trail passes near the vermin-proof fence, built to help conserve wildlife, and there is a pedestrian access gate. This area can be inundated during winter.
4   Areas cleared of vegetation reflect past disturbance and current grazing by rabbits. The fence should help to control this problem and allow the natural vegetation to regrow.
5   The trail moves into reed beds with occasional glimpses to the lake. Wetland vegetation is more evident than on the western side and wading birds are more common during winter. Rushes can give visual protection to visitors wanting to watch the birds without disturbing them. The track along this eastern edge becomes waterlogged during winter.

Tracy Churchill, Annabelle Vowels

Where is it? *34 km south of Perth. Entrance at Russell Road, between Pearse Road and Hammond Road.*
Travelling time: *30 minutes from Perth via Kwinana Freeway, Forrest Road and Hammond Road.*
Facilities: *Carpark.*
On-site information: *Information shelter at entrance.*
Best season: *Spring, autumn.*

Index by walk length

Length(return)	Name	Region	Walk No.
5 km	Claremont Foreshore Trail	River	31
5 km	The Spectacles Walktrail	South	47
5 km	Zamia Trail	North	29
5.2 km	Four Seasons Trail	River	32
5.7 km	Thomsons Lake Trail	South	48
6 km	Bibra Lake Walk	South	39
7 km	Mt Vincent Walktrail	South	44
7.5 km	Yaberoo Budjara Heritage Trail – Wagardu Lake to Pipidinny	North	27
8 km*	Valley to Valley Walk	Hills	10
8.5 km	Kingfisher Trail	North	19
9.2 km	Ghost House Trail	North	14
10 km	Between the Bridges Walk	River	30
10.2 km	John Forrest Heritage Trail	Hills	2
10.6 km	Echidna Trail	North	13
12 km	Abyssinia Rock Walktrail	South	37
18 km	King Jarrah Track	South	41

*One-way (Best walked from south to north.)

CALM offices

State Operations Headquarters
20 Dick Perry Avenue
Technology Park, Western Precinct
KENSINGTON 6151
Phone (08) 9334 0333
Fax (08) 9334 0466

Tracks and Trails Unit
Phone (08) 9334 0265
email: bibtrack@calm.wa.gov.au

Swan Regional Office
20 Dick Perry Avenue
Technology Park, Western Precinct
KENSINGTON 6151
Phone (08) 9368 4399
Fax (08) 9368 4299

CALM Outdoors Information Centre
40 Jull Street
ARMADALE 6112
Phone (08) 9399 9746
Fax (08) 9399 9748

District Offices
Perth Hills:
Mundaring Weir Road
MUNDARING 6073
Phone (08) 9295 1955
Fax (08) 9295 2404

Swan Coastal:
5 Dundebar Road
WANNEROO 6065
Phone (08) 9405 0700
Fax (08) 9405 0777

Dwellingup Work Centre:
Banksiadale Road
DWELLINGUP 6213
Phone (08) 9538 1078
Fax (08) 9538 1203

Fremantle Work Centre:
47 Henry Street
FREMANTLE
Phone (08) 9336 0111
Fax (08) 9430 5408

PLEASE NOTE:
CALM does not have an after hours number. If you have a genuine emergency while bushwalking (for example, a serious injury to one of your party) you should contact the Police on 000.

Discovery books

Discovering the Swan River and the Swan Estuary Marine Park
A pocket-sized lucky dip into the Swan River and its activities – windsurfing, diving, walking, cycling and more. With photos, maps and descriptions of walks and dive sites.

Discovering Yanchep National Park
Submerse yourself in the history, heritage, bushland, wildlife and wetlands of one of Western Australia's oldest and most popular national parks.

Discovering Nambung National Park
Delves into the geology and formation of the park's centrepiece, the amazing Pinnacles, and much more besides. Features a self-guided drive trail from Cervantes to the Pinnacles.

Discovering Shark Bay Marine Park and Monkey Mia
Come face to face with dolphins in a remarkable World Heritage Area! Whale sharks, turtles and dugongs are just a few of the inhabitants of a seascape like no other.

Discovering Penguin Island and the Shoalwater Islands Marine Park
Less than an hour's drive from Perth is one of the State's most delightful natural areas, also a playground for fairy penguins, sea lions, dolphins and other marine life. Includes a self-guided walk around Penguin Island.

Discovering the Valley of the Giants and the Walpole-Nornalup National Park
Walk through the canopy of ancient giants, the rare tingle trees. This book has information on bushwalking, fishing, camping, whale watching and four-wheel-driving in and around the park.

Discovery books retail for only $6.50.

Bush Books

This series of full-colour pocket guides features WA's very own plants, animals and special features. They're comprehensive, accurate, interesting and informative. There are 31 titles so far...

Orchids of the South-West
Threatened and Rare Birds of Western Australia
Bugs in the Backyard
Western Australian Birds of Prey
Beachcombers Guide to South-West Beaches
Trees of the Goldfields
Bush Tucker Plants of the South-West
Wildflowers of Shark Bay
Geology and Landforms of the Kimberley
Plants of the Pilbara
Animals of Shark Bay
Wildflowers of the South Coast
Wildflowers of the Mid-West
Wildflowers of the South-West Forests
Mammals of the South-West
Whales and Dolphins of Western Australia
Common Trees of the South-West Forests
Birds in the Backyard
Birds of the South-West Forests
Plants of the Kimberley
Mammals of North-Western Australia
Hazardous Animals of North-Western Australia
Birds of the Kimberley
Waterbirds of South-West Wetlands
Threatened Wildflowers of the Mid-West
Geology and Landforms of the South-West
Fungi of the South-West Forests
Frogs of Western Australian
Wildflowers of the Stirling Range
Geology and Landforms of the Pilbara
Wildflowers of Dryandra Woodland

Bush Books are inexpensive, with a recommended retail price of just $6.50.

Let us tell you where to go!